Praise for
Be Queen of Your Life

A delightful follow-up to *The Gospel According to Mamma,* I found this book full of darned good advice for those days I'm the queen...and the many I still feel like the princess...and many reminders of conversations I should have with the two princesses in my realm as they struggle onward. It would make a great addition to any book club reading list, especially those that cherish spirituality and the teachings of the Bible.

—Meg Welch Dendler
author of *Why Kimba Saved The World*
and mother of two teenage daughters

So many times advice books offer a well-meaning anchor... which weighs you down. Happily, Annette Bridges' advice to young women is the opposite -- it's uplifting and, well, actually *fun*. Inspired by her own ups and downs as her daughter left home, married, divorced, and started life anew, Bridges recognizes that God always has our best interests at heart. Bridges' breezy stories, based on experience and analyzed with common sense and gentle faith, will win smiles from daughters... and mothers, sisters, nieces everywhere.

—Julie Hedgepeth Williams
author of *A Rare Titanic Family: The Caldwells' Story of Survival*

Don't be fooled by Annette Bridges' homespun prose—there is genuine wisdom in this book, not just for mothers and daughters, but for everyone. One has to admire her courage and generosity in revealing some very personal incidents simply because she knew they might help someone.

—Amy H. Duncan
author of *Getting Down to Brass Tacks - My adventures in the world of jazz, Rio, and beyond*

Take a day and go to the beach, mountains or wherever you find inspiration and read, *Be Queen of Your Life*. If I were asked to sum up this book in one word it would be honesty. It is a brutally honest look at the author's life and lessons learned. What I appreciated was the way it got me to rethink some of the challenges in my own experience and how to find solutions. Her description of self-pity as "wounded ego" gave me plenty to be honest about in my own life. I loved thinking about the seven wonders being to see, hear, feel, touch, taste, laugh and love vs. places and things. It turned my thought to gratitude instead of regret or despair over lost opportunities. Annette writes with poignancy, depth and humor. It will start the 'mental wheels turning' and perhaps move you forward when you have felt stuck in life. Well done!

—Connie Pierce
author of *My Journey of Real Life Weight Loss: How I Lost Over 180 pounds*

This book is a highly engaging and entertaining advice book perfect for young women setting out on their own. Whether you are going to college, getting married, experiencing a divorce or starting life anew, *Be Queen of Your Life* has something for you.

—Jennifer Bridges
Ph.D. student and Annette's sassy southern daughter

Be Queen of Your Life

A savvy mom helps daughters command and rule their lives

Also by Annette Bridges

The Gospel According to Mamma:
  One mother's philosophy on love, money, God, aging, decisions, change, and much more

Have Lipstick, Will Travel
  How to reimagine your life, purpose & hair color

Lady and Bella
  Totally different, Totally friends

Lady and Bella's Alphabet Kitchen
  A to Z Recipes for Kid Cooks

Be Queen of Your Life

A savvy mom helps daughters command and rule their lives

ANNETTE BRIDGES

Be Queen of Your Life
© 2013 by Ranch House Press. All rights reserved.
Printed in the United States of America.

www.annettebridges.com

ISBN-13: 978-0-9976014-1-1

*To Jennifer Rae Bridges,
the young woman I'm proud to call my daughter.
You are this mom's greatest blessing!*

"The art of mothering is to teach the art of living..."
Elaine Heffner
GoodEnoughMothering.com

Contents

xi | Overview

1 | Part One: Off to college

31 | Part Two: Marriage

65 | Part Three: Divorce and other drama

111 | Part Four: Going for goals

139 | Part Five: The rest of your life

171 | Afterword

174 | Featured quotes

180 | Acknowledgments

Overview

Be the queen of your own life! That's the call to action of the book you hold in your hands. It's filled with plenty of advice, tips, and lessons learned from my own lifelong transition to queen-hood.

While any woman can benefit from reading and implementing the wisdom shared, my hope is that *Be Queen of Your Life* makes its way into the hands of young women—especially teenagers and college students.

My daughter always told me I gave good advice. After she set out on her own in college and then in marriage, she started telling me my advice was "darn good." I'm flattered to say that in her eyes, I am her queen of darn good advice!

In this book you'll read about my daughter's first ten years away from home. It was her encounters and challenges during those years that influenced this book's framework. Like my daughter's life, the book flows through five parts: "Off to College," "Marriage," "Divorce and Other Drama," "Going for Goals," and "The Rest of Your Life." However, the individual essays are not confined to those topics. In other words, even if you've not dealt with a divorce, you can still benefit from reading "Banish Debbie Downer from the realm" or from "Princesses rice and shine—never rise and whine."

The fifty-plus essays presented in this book are a collection of memoirs from my life that show how I overcame and defeated dragons of dilemmas and disasters. My words are not mere theory and wishful thinking. They are "been there, done that" kinds of stories. They are true confessions and honest admissions that are not always easy for me to share. But I share them anyway!

I believe we women need to share our epiphanies with one another, encourage each other, and build a strong sisterhood in a world too often ruled by those who would tear us apart. This book is about you. It's about building a relationship with the one who should always be your first true love—yourself.

If you're struggling with procrastination, shyness, discouragement, depression, pessimism, over-reacting, self-pity, regret, bad grades, bad days, mistakes, envy, jealousy, sexual harassment, death, in-law problems, money problems, not enough time, or unwanted change, or looking for a happy relationship, more fun and happiness, forgiveness, more hope, more gratitude, new dreams, and a better attitude and self-image, you're opening the right book!

Girls, you are the queen of your own lives. You have the power you need to command and rule your world. Your power begins with your attitude. And your attitude, my darlings, is unstoppable and invincible! It is your shield that protects and sustains you. Are you ready to learn how to use it to reach your dreams and accomplish your goals? Let's get started!

Part One
Off to college

3 | Introduction
5 | Look for a country boy to be your prince
8 | Even kings can't read minds
11 | The "Are you my prince?" method may not work
15 | Love or hate—choose well, princesses
19 | Queens get it done today
22 | A supportive friend is true royalty
25 | Sometimes princesses must speak up
28 | Let the princess within come forth

Off to college—Introduction

I couldn't stop the clock. My world changed September 2001 when my only child—my daughter, my princess—headed off to college.

You have to understand—Jennifer is not only my daughter. She is also my shopping companion, my movie buddy, and my confidante. She is my best friend. When Jennifer was born, I stopped teaching school to be an at-home mom. When she started school, I went back to teaching at her elementary school. In fact, I was her kindergarten teacher.

In Jennifer's fifth-grade year, we started home schooling and continued through high school. It was a good fit for our cattle-ranching lifestyle. She and I loved learning together. Besides, it left us plenty of time to travel as a family, something I couldn't even imagine doing without our daughter. Even when she went to summer camp, I went with her and volunteered.

I suspect I'm not the only mother who struggled with sleepless nights and anxious days after their daughter left home. My little princess was about to begin her own life journey. It was inevitable, and I knew I had to face it. The time had finally arrived for me to let her go—without going with her. It was time for me to become queen of the next chapter in my life—life without a child at home, also known as being an "empty nester."

So yes, my world did change that September. But I eventually learned that I didn't have to be afraid of change. Change can bring progress, encourage growth, and provide more expansive views. My change was like the transformation of a caterpillar to a butterfly. Day-to-day life may have shifted, but what a difference in the view!

What of my little princess? She readily embraced her new life and had many wonderful experiences in college. She completed her bachelor's of the arts degree in three years. She went on to complete two master's degrees and will soon be adding a Ph.D. to her educational achievements.

I had many words of wisdom to give her as she left home. So here begins my "Off to College" suggestions. These are not exhaustive by any means, but they attempt to cover some of the essentials I hope many daughters will find helpful.

Look for a country boy to be your prince

I don't think young women today head off to college with the same goal that I had in 1976. My priority was to find the man I would marry. After attending the largest high school in Dallas, I was going to a small private college surrounded by young men I thought shared my same values. I thought it would be the ideal setting to meet the perfect husband.

I was wrong.

After six years of only dating city boys at high school and college, I met a country boy after I returned home at twenty-two, when I least expected it. I guess this is why it was easy for me to recommend to my daughter that her best hopes for her Prince Charming would come in dating a country boy. What I should have explained better is that it's not only boys raised in the country who are good boyfriend material. It's the qualities the man embodies that make him a prince.

The qualities my husband John expressed made him a wonderful boyfriend and, later, a great husband and daddy. The things that matter most when looking for a good man are his qualities and not so much his appearance or the geography of his hometown.

When I think of my husband, I think of the country song by Trace Adkins, "Ladies Love Country Boys." I couldn't agree more! But why did I fall in love with my country boy?

My mamma raised me to be a "lady," just like the song says of its heroine. Most of my growing up years were spent in the big cities of Atlanta and Dallas, where I attended the largest schools. Although I went to that small private college, all the boys I met were also from big cities. My youthful years were filled with theater, dance, musicals, and symphony. Most of my college weekends were spent disco dancing.

Perhaps you can imagine my mamma's surprise when I announced I was marrying a country boy from a small North Texas town and was going to live on his family's cattle ranch. She often joked that she didn't raise me to get my hands dirty, so she had a difficult time imagining her princess living in the country.

John actually grew up in the big city of Dallas, but his parents bought the ranch when he was five years old. He spent most weekends and summers of his growing up years in the country doing what country boys do—hauling hay, working cattle, hunting, fishing, getting sweaty and dirty, and loving it. They moved to the country full-time after he graduated from high school. My husband grew up with the love of the country in his mind, body, and soul. There was never any question where he and his wife would live after he married.

So what are the qualities I consider as requisite in a prince?

Good manners, dependability, and honesty are the first three that occur to me. My man always says "please" when he asks me to do something and "thank you" afterwards. When he makes a promise, he keeps it. When he says he will do something, he does it. When you need his help, he's ready and willing. When he gives you a compliment, he means it. He doesn't throw compliments around casually, mind you. If you need the truth, ask him, and the truth is what you'll get. It may not be exactly what you want to hear, but he gives his honest opinion and viewpoint in a gentle and kind manner.

My man is also sincere, trustworthy, candid, straightforward, plainspoken, genuine, truehearted, and square shooting. Oh yeah, did I say my sweet man is patient? One of my favorite daddy/daughter memories with our toddler daughter was when John came in the house after a long, hot day working outside. He would immediately be greeted by our sweet little girl, who had comb and spray-bottle in hand, ready to give her daddy what she called a "wet and wild" hairdo. Of course her daddy obliged her request. He'd sit on the floor and get his new "do" no matter how tired he was—day after day.

Turns out that "country boy" is synonymous for "good man." When I say look for a country boy, I'm saying look for a good man—a prince who has a calm nature and endearing personality. Consider what qualities are most important to you, and keep your gaze on men who express and live those qualities. These men are not only good mate material, but they make good friends, too.

Even kings can't read minds

I doubt I'm the only woman who ever wished her man could read her mind. I can't count the times, especially in the early years of my marriage, when I lamented, "Just once, could he know what I'm feeling or what I need without my explaining it to him or writing him a book?"

Sorry to tell you this, ladies, but not even Superman could read minds, much to Lois Lane's dismay.

I spent more than a couple of years in anguish and agony over my husband's inability to understand what I was thinking. It never occurred to me that I couldn't read his thoughts either, so why did I ever imagine—or hope—he could read mine?

I knew a couple who were married for almost seventy years. The wife wrote her husband weekly letters explaining to him—in infinite detail—her feelings, frustrations, and longings. I used to think it was a funny thing to do. But it seemed to work well for them. I don't know if he ever wrote her letters, but at least she was communicating her thoughts with him.

Too many years of my marriage went by before my communication skills with my husband began to improve. Why was it so hard to talk with him about my innermost feelings? Many days I spent crying that he didn't understand me. But how could he without my making an effort to help him?

Perhaps the place to get to in a marriage, or any relationship, is the desire to understand your man as much as you want him to understand you.

Webster defines communication as "a process by which information is exchanged between individuals." "Exchanged" is the key word in this definition to me, as it suggests two parties exchanging—communicating—with each other.

Another definition of communication is "the exchange of thoughts, messages or information by speech, signals, writing, or behavior." From my experience, speech and writing have been more effective at getting my point across than signals or behavior.

For example, every time I tried the "silent treatment" when I was upset about something and went to bed in that mode, my husband just thought I was sleepy. He would go on to sleep while I lay there half the night stewing. When I would wake him—eventually—he would be totally clueless that anything was wrong.

Signals can get crossed, which then results in a mutual misunderstanding—or, in other words, a failure to communicate. Using words to effectively impart information could be considered an "art"—as another definition of communication suggested.

There seems to be an art in how we say what we want to say. Implementing the proper use of tone and emphasis as well as body language when speaking are significant factors in getting our meaning across correctly. Without the correct usage, however, the "recipient" in the exchange could become defensive or get hurt feelings as well as totally misunderstand the meaning the "sender" intended.

I would not say I've mastered the art of communicating with my husband, although I'm much better after thirty-plus years of marriage. Of course, it could be that women really are from Venus and men from Mars, so we're destined to never completely understand each other. But recognizing that men and women have different needs and communicate in different ways is a good way to begin.

It's important to realize that words can have different meanings to men and women. I once heard a comedian explain this. He gave the word "communication" as an example. He said women define communication as "the open sharing of thoughts and feelings with one's partner." Men define it as "leaving a note before taking a fishing trip with the boys."

Alas, without the ability to read each other's minds, kings and queens may never be able to completely understand each other. But we'll never get better without trying. That takes some form of communication. When it comes to communicating with our boyfriends or husbands, you will probably find, as I have, that practice goes a long way toward mastering this skill.

The "Are you my prince?" method may not work

Looking for your Mr. Right may sometimes seem like a futile journey. Some suggest that too many of us are clueless about what we want or need and claim this is the reason we don't find a permanent partner.

Many of us would say our love life has not always been a bed of roses. I suspect at least some of us have been dumped more times than we want to say. I wish someone had told me, "He's just not that into you!" These words of wisdom might have kept me from wasting so many days (or weeks) pining over what I thought was lost love. Indeed, I traveled many miles on the road from rejection to romance before I met my husband.

I recall one breakup that occurred weeks before I admitted it. I was home from college working one semester while my boyfriend was still in school. Apparently, he thought our distance apart meant we were free to date others. But I remained faithful, thinking we would pick up where we left off when I returned to school. I went up to visit school during that semester off, and neither he nor any of my girlfriends let me know he was dating another girl. Eventually, one of my girlfriends told me. I felt so betrayed, humiliated, and foolish.

Rejection can leave you feeling devastated. It can seem impossible to get past the hurt. At such times I wanted to withdraw into my little private castle and hide away from the world. But time heals all wounds, and I eventually got back in the saddle—at least until I was thrown off the horse again. However, after a fall, many folks advise: "Dust yourself off and get back on the horse."

Some people promise you're most likely to find Mr. Right when you're not looking for him. This was what happened to me. But just because I wasn't specifically looking for my prince at Six Flags Over Texas one hot summer day didn't mean I wasn't a hopeful romantic and very expectant that Mr. Right would cross my path someday.

I had spent my dating years implementing the "Are you my prince?" method. Remember the Dr. Seuss Beginner Book, *Are You My Mother?* A baby bird hatches while his mother is away. After falling from his nest, the confused little bird sets out to find his mother and asks everyone he meets the big question—including a dog, a cow, and even an airplane. ("How could I be your mother?" said the cow. "I am a cow.")

Every man I dated was evaluated with my big question in mind. After a few years of unsuccessful hunting by this method, I came to the realization that too much analysis caused me to miss out on a lot of fun and friendships, and, in the end, I still hadn't found my prince.

About a year before I met my husband, I decided I needed a new approach to my pursuit of lasting romance. A relationship with a boyfriend had come to a bitter end after a year of steady dating, so I took a "timeout." When I met my husband,

I had not dated anyone in over a year. During my sabbatical, I realized that most of my previous relationships ended because of my own insecurities and possessiveness. I concluded that I needed some time to refocus on my goals and get a better sense of my own life purpose and identity as an independent woman.

Friends and my mamma advised me to focus on living a full and happy life rather than searching desperately for a husband. "Do things you like to do and you'll meet others who love to do the same as you," they said. This sounded like good advice, and indeed it resulted in many quality friendships with both men and women. My obsessive search for a prince no longer monopolized my thoughts.

Some say the key to getting off the dating merry-go-round requires nothing more than taking the time to get to know yourself before you try to get to know someone else. Indeed! For the first time in my young womanhood, I thought about my interests and career goals and even explored new hobbies.

I believe that God, who I think of as divine Mother Love, peoples the world so none of us have to be alone. We're walking this life journey together—side by side. (I love pondering the feminine nature of the Divine, so in this book I'll sometimes refer to God as "Mother," "Love," and "She.") Even though I wasn't in a dating relationship, I spent more time than ever before with many different people as I made new friendships.

So don't waste time in dismay if your Mr. Today turns out not to be your Mr. Forever. If you've not yet met your Mr. Right, stop the search. I met my prince when I least expected. I wasn't looking for him, but I was busy enjoying myself and making friends. I was happy and satisfied already—which is probably what attracted him to me. I think I could have remained happy and lived a fulfilling life even if I had not met my husband.

Maybe there would have been a great career or lifework ahead of me. That would have been a good thing, too.

Love or hate—choose well, princesses

You may not need me to remind you to love your enemies, those with different viewpoints, or those who are difficult to work with. But trust me, in college you're going to meet many people who don't share your opinion or values. This fact will remain true the rest of your life. It's important to be prepared to make responsible choices and learn how to get along even with those you don't like or who don't like you.

Have you ever heard the 1972 song, "Why Can't We Live Together?" written by Timmy Thomas? The song's title and lyrics ask a poignant, timeless question for individuals, schools, communities, and even nations when struggling with mistrust, resentment, and deep-seated hatred.

Why can't we live together? It's a question I have often asked myself when watching turmoil reported on the news. I recall one such report from Jena, Louisiana, on the "Jena 6." Back in 2006, six black high school students were charged with attempted murder (later the charges were reduced) following a schoolyard fight with one white student.

But that was not the beginning of the story. A few months before the fight, a black student sat under a tree in the schoolyard where white students normally congregated. The following day, three nooses hung from the tree. School officials responded with a three-day suspension for the white students who'd put up the nooses. These incidents only fueled the mounting racial tension that had long been plaguing the community.

The Jena 6 news story reminded me of when I was fourteen years old and caught in the middle of the hatred and divisiveness that came with the hot-button issue of the time—racial integration in my Texas high school.

I believed that God loves each one of us equally. My mamma and I often talked about how Divine Love doesn't see differences in her children, but instead sees unique qualities. I knew that I, too, needed to appreciate the uniqueness of each of God's children, instead of focusing on differences. After all, we shared a common bond since we had the same divine parent. These ideas were the basis of my prayers and thoughts. I had empathy for my new classmates making long bus trips to school each morning.

One day, a small group of white students began loudly sharing their negative opinions about our new classmates—or so I was later told. Unfortunately, a few of the voices came from my fellow drill team members. As I entered the gym for team practice, I found myself in the middle of an argument between white drill team members and black female students. Suddenly, a tennis racket was hurled through the air and inadvertently hit me in the face.

Although I hadn't done anything to provoke this, I was caught in the middle of a heated division. But I wasn't about to allow myself to get sucked into anger or hatred. I didn't want to choose sides. I had no idea what had prompted the exchange since I only arrived on the scene after the tennis racket was mid-air. The choice, as I saw it, even after being hit in the face, was to love. I could love my fellow drill team members, the new students in the gym, and even the girl who threw the racket.

My choice was based on what I had learned from reading stories in the Bible. In its pages, there were many examples that illustrated the futility and dire consequences of hatred. In the New Testament, Jesus was the ultimate role model for responding to discrimination and injustice—both in his actions and in his teachings.

It was unfair that he was arrested and treated like a criminal. Some could say his disciples were justified in fighting the guards who came to take him away before his crucifixion; some might even praise the disciple who cut off one of the guard's ears. But not Jesus! He rebuked the violent act and restored the guard's ear with compassion.

I also agreed with the conclusion of nineteenth-century author on spirituality Mary Baker Eddy. She wrote that hatred "is a plague-spot that spreads its virus and kills at last...if indulged, it masters us." Hatred was a virus I could defend myself against. I didn't want any part of it. Clearly, to me, the remedy was love. If I harbored hate, I'd be duped into seeing my classmates as less than the ideal, beloved children of God. But praying from the basis that there was one Divine Love animating and empowering us could bring real change and reform.

I walked away from that incident in that gym with the confidence that Mother Love would prevail if only we could keep trying to be friends and get to know each other. (I suffered no permanent harm from being hit by the racket.) Over the next few years, I witnessed the progress that took place at my school. Even though things got worse for a while—more fights and police guarding hallways and school grounds—by my senior year, there was increased harmony. Friendships between the races did develop. My drill team was integrated, as well as the other clubs and sports teams at the school. I could feel intolerance giving way to mutual respect and understanding—and I felt I'd played a small part by making the conscious choice to be loving. This meant not passing judgment or making assumptions and not partaking in gossip or bullying, but being willing to be a friend and to be respectful and sensitive toward the feelings of others.

The need and desire to actively practice this kind of love on a daily basis can take some work. But I believe we are all more than equipped for the task. Bitterness and hatred aren't self-sustaining because they lack the support of the only perpetuating force in the universe—Love. With Love at the forefront of how we live, it's difficult to have enemies. Endeavoring to understand one another from the basis of our relationship to God brings healing to the darkest of situations. It dispels fear and sets us on the clearest path to reconciliation and unity

Remember, since you're royalty, to love or to hate is yours to decide.

Queens get it done today

If my daughter takes after her mom, to stop procrastinating would be easier said than done. Since I was born in Georgia, Scarlett O'Hara's famous words, "Tomorrow is another day," run deep in my blood. But my mamma never threatened, "No dessert until you eat your veggies," so I've had to work hard to come up with incentives to do whatever it is that I'm avoiding.

Procrastination has its roots in Latin, meaning "in favor of tomorrow." The fact is, most of the time, it's not a matter of my wanting to wait until tomorrow—or next week or next year—to do whatever it is. Usually when I put something off, I regret that I did.

In college, I was one of those students who pulled "all-nighters" to write my papers. Sometimes—miraculously—they turned out pretty good. But then there were other times when I'm sure I could have done a better job if I had not been so rushed. In either case, I never enjoyed the stress and pressure I put myself under. But I did eventually get better at my time management.

It's been many years since my college days, but I do still have occasions when I come up with some elaborate reasons about how "now just isn't a good time."

I think there are many reasons why we put off until tomorrow what we could do today. Who doesn't want to avoid unpleasant tasks? Or perhaps some things just feel too difficult? Sometimes we put off long enough to make it impossible to do a good job. Then we have a handy excuse for failure since we just didn't have enough time.

The two things I avoid most of all are laundry and doing our income tax. I know they need to be done. I know I have to do them. But surely tomorrow will be a better day!

There have been many more things, however, that I hate to admit I've put off. My best intentions would be to call old friends, then many times it ended up never happening. Sadly, days, months, years passed until friendships became only memories.

There are other things I wanted to stop putting off such as exercising, going for a walk, reading a new book, having lunch with a friend, and finishing a project—to name a few. There were trips to take or the diet to begin if I would only stop putting them off till someday in the future. I eventually discovered that I was spending more time feeling bad about avoiding a task or project than it would have taken to complete it.

I recall a time when a new friend was soon to move away and I was sad we had not gotten to know one another earlier. I realized how lost opportunities come about when we don't live more in the moment and make the most of each one. I finally understood that tomorrow isn't always a possibility. I adopted a new goal on how to approach my life.

An opportunity came for me to implement my new goal. Another good friend had moved away a few years earlier. We had seen each other on occasion since. But for years we talked about going on a trip together—just us girls. Every time she asked me,

I had some reason why I couldn't. So when she called to invite me to join her and another friend on a trip to Italy, she was certain I would again have an excuse on why I couldn't. I had my passport, so that could not be my reason. I had never been to Europe nor had I been on a vacation without my husband. I had plenty of fears about flying across the ocean. But when I called my friend back, after giving this opportunity some serious consideration, I told her I had already purchased my plane tickets, much to her surprise and delight. Our fabulous trip to Italy was followed by an exciting trip to Switzerland and Austria a few months later—again without husbands.

My message to all queens and princesses everywhere is the same message I say to myself these days: Stop putting things off! No more regrets! There is no better time than the present to be with our friends and family. Why add needless stress to our lives by putting everything off until tomorrow? Today is a good day, too!

A supportive friend is true royalty

My friend Shirley was also a friend to my daughter. I can't give any recommendations to my daughter—any daughters—on how to be a good friend without talking about Shirley. Since college provides many wonderful opportunities to develop life-long friendships, I hope introducing my friend to you ladies helps you learn how to be a better friend yourself.

A few years ago Shirley lost her battle with cancer. She transitioned to the next road on her eternal journey. But before she left, she taught me much about what it means to be a friend.

The memorial service held in her honor was attended by a large congregation of family, friends, and colleagues. An awe-inspiring moment for me was when one of Shirley's former colleagues from twenty-eight years ago stood up to speak. As he began, he said he was sure no one in the crowded room had ever seen him before. He explained that he had worked for a Houston newspaper with Shirley. At some point, he had an opportunity to go to the Middle East to be a correspondent, and apparently Shirley was a voice of encouragement amid a deep sea of disapproval. He shared that it was her encouragement that helped him make a career decision that changed his life, and he would be forever grateful to her. He remains an international correspondent.

My friend Shirley was an encourager. I, too, have been blessed by her emboldening and motivating words. If I was bewildered, confused, uncertain, doubt-filled, or frustrated, her encouragement was there.

Shirley's reassurance was not limited only to difficult times, but also, as her newspaper colleague expressed, to times of possibility when her cheering and boosting were perhaps the greatest. I think Shirley saw each of her friends, family, and colleagues as on the road to reaching their full potential, and she knew encouragement would help us on that journey. She gave it abundantly. The inspiriting atmosphere that filled our conversations allowed me to think aloud when I was with her. Every dialogue was one of self-discovery, and I was changed by each and every visit. She saw the best in me and helped me to see it, too.

Einstein describes friendship in this way: "Only a life lived for others is a life worthwhile." We read in the Bible book of John, "Greater love hath no man than this, that a man lay down his life for his friends" (John 15:13). Proverbs 17:17 says, "A friend loveth at all times." Author Mary Baker Eddy sums up friendship by saying it brings "to earth a foretaste of heaven." Indeed!

My good friend Shirley gave her life for her friends—giving her time, imparting her passion, contributing her energy, offering her ideas, bestowing her inspiration. A synonym for "giver" is "angel." I believe there are angels among us, and they're also known as friends.

Shirley encouraged me to follow my heart, my dreams, my vision, my inspiration. I hope to encourage my daughter—all daughters—to do the same. I hope I make as much of a difference in my daughter's life—and in your life—as Shirley has in mine.

May each of us never underestimate the power of encouraging words and always share them lavishly and bountifully with our friends and loved ones, as well as with our acquaintances and even strangers. We make a difference in the lives of others—often much more than we'll ever know.

Sometimes princesses must speak up

When we're children and tell our mother what a sibling did or a teacher what a fellow student did, people say we tattled. But by the time we're in college, no matter how good we were at tattling as a child, we sometimes forget there are times when we need to speak up about the actions of another.

Being the youngest in my family with three big brothers, I always seemed to find something to tattle about. Was my tattling a ploy to get attention? I suspect so—at least some of the time.

Whatever my reason, some might say my childhood job was to be the family informer. I usually tattled because I was mad at one of my brothers and I wanted to get him in trouble. Of course, this particular brother usually had done something worthy of getting in trouble. I just passed along the incriminating information.

Many children fear the label of rat, squealer, fink, or blabbermouth, but there are things children should feel free and comfortable to tell.

Children may be embarrassed or ashamed of the inappropriate behavior someone has done toward them. Their confusion can make them hold their tongue when they should in fact tell what was done.

Sometimes our friends confide in us, and it can be difficult for us to know the difference between secrets that we should keep and those that we need to share with another.

I had a childhood friend who vowed me to secrecy about an adult's inappropriate sexual behavior toward her. I have to tell you that her secret was one I kept her entire life. My friend passed on several years ago, but I'm still sad because she may have endured much pain and unhappiness and I never did anything to stop it.

It had been so easy for me to snitch on my brothers. Yet I can't explain why I couldn't blab about my friend's experience to my mother or some other authority figure.

When I think back on all the tattling I did on my brothers, I think that in fact the brother in question was doing things that he shouldn't have been doing—drinking beer and smoking marijuana to name two. At the time I didn't understand why I needed to tell on him—that it wasn't to get him into trouble but to help him stop doing things that were harmful to his health.

We all need to learn the difference between senseless tattling and a legitimate complaint or concern. As in many areas of our lives, an examination of our motives is paramount.

Is what we feel compelled to share something that affects ours or others' physical or psychological safety? Is our motive the intent to protect? Is there an emergency—when danger is imminent?

When I was eleven, I had a friend tattle on me that resulted in my suspension from school for three days. This was in 1969 when the hippie movement was popular among youth. Part of this culture was taking drugs and getting "high." I didn't have access to "real" drugs, but I did take some prescription pills from a bottle that belonged to my mamma. I took these to school and pretended they were a drug to make you happy. I even offered one to my friend. Thankfully, neither of us took the medication. But my friend told our teacher about my "happy pills." I don't think I ever thanked this friend for her brave actions. It was clearly her concern for my safety as well as that of others that she snitched. I was at first humiliated and angry. But I can tell you now that her tattling completely altered my life. I was forced to make some changes that put me on a better path.

We all need to learn how to evaluate and process information so we know what's important and how and when to tattle. It took me a few missed opportunities of not tattling when I was in college before I learned that tattling wasn't just for kids.

Twice I had conversations with young men who eventually committed suicide. I don't know if it would have made a difference if I had told someone my concerns about them. Suicide wasn't a thought in my head either time, but I did feel they were troubled and needed some kind of help. Another time, I was being stalked by a young man I had one date with but never another because I was uncomfortable and uneasy around him. Instead of saying anything to anyone about the weird notes he was leaving me on my car windshield, I changed jobs, phone numbers, and my residence in the hopes he couldn't find me again. Yet another time, I had a professor try to sell me a good grade for sexual favors. I never reported him to the proper authorities.

After many guilt-ridden years, I finally came to grips with my inactions and forgave myself for my lapses in judgment in these instances, vowing to never make the same misjudgments again. I should have spoken up. I did, however, finally understand that there is always a right time to tattle.

Let the princess within come forth

How often I have looked at other women and compared myself to them? In my early childhood, many times I wanted to ask a girl to come over to play at my house, but I didn't. I thought, *Why would she want to come to my house? Her house was so much bigger and prettier.* No doubt there were many friendships I missed out on because of my own feelings of inferiority.

In high school, comparisons were inevitable and not always by choice. Social cliques were delineated by those who were on the cheerleading or drill teams and those who were not, the pretty girls and the plain girls, the skinny girls and the fat girls, the smart girls and the, shall we say, academically challenged girls, as well as the designer-dressed girls and the bargain-basement girls. It was very clear how you stacked up and to which group you belonged.

After many school years of comparing as an acceptable mode of behavior, perhaps it's no surprise that, as adults, we continue to compare ourselves with our neighbors, friends, and colleagues. The problem with comparing is that it often leads to envy, jealousy, unnecessary competitiveness, and an undermining of our own self-worth.

In fact, comparing oneself with others is the basis for the old adage, "The grass is always greener on the other side of the fence." We believe others are always in a better situation than we are, although they may not be. I can recall an instance when I was envious of a friend of mine because I thought her life was much easier, that she had fewer problems to contend with, and that she was more satisfied with her life than I was with mine. As is often the case when making assumptions, I was wrong.

Measuring ourselves against others sours our life, creating anxiety, stress, isolation, and depression. It is a fruitless exercise and an incredible waste of energy. The truth is, there's no one like us, and this makes us incomparable.

We're each one of a kind with different traits, talents, skills, and abilities. Each of us has God-given special gifts. We have our own life purpose to fulfill. No one can do a better job of being you than you.

As a middle-aged woman, I grew weary of fretting about someone else's funnier jokes or her smaller bottom or her newer car or her bigger paycheck or her flatter stomach and so on and so on. I finally tired of feeling inadequate and not good enough.

On our cattle ranch, I've seen fields rich with green grass with always that one cow who would rather risk getting her head stuck between barbed-wire to eat grass on the other side of the fence than to eat what's right at her feet. The grass truly wasn't any greener or better. In fact, the grass on the other side of the fence had not received the fertilizer the grass in the hayfields had received and truly wasn't as good and nutritious. I decided that perhaps I spent too many years like that silly cow, not recognizing the good at hand in my own self.

Comparing myself with other women and concluding that I didn't measure up actually kept me from being friends with some cool ladies. I have no doubt that I missed out on what could have been some great friendships. When I finally stopped all the comparing, I made some new friends who became dear and precious to me. I stopped being so harsh on myself, too. It turns out that many of my comparisons were the result of my own lack of self-appreciation. Being kinder, patient, and more tolerant of myself helped me believe I could do something about some of the things I didn't like and resulted in my getting that smaller bottom and flatter stomach.

In his first letter to the Corinthians in the Bible, Paul gives an insightful and helpful analogy on the futility of comparing. He describes one body having many different parts, illustrating the importance and uniqueness of each one. Each of these parts has a valuable role—not one is better or less important than another. While all are different from the others, all are united into one body (1 Corinthians 12:12–26).

Pondering this beautiful analogy helped me recognize my uniqueness and special gifts and, consequently, also value and appreciate who I am—what makes me a "second to none" me. I suspect we all can do a much better job being ourselves than attempting to be someone else. So, princess, tell yourself as you head off to college, "Why not just be the best possible me instead of a poor imitation of her?"

Part Two
Marriage

33 | Introduction
37 | Jealousy is the dragon
40 | Majestic communication and the Golden Rule
43 | When your prince surprises you, go with it
46 | It's not all about tiaras and scepters
49 | Find beauty in the kingdom by opening your eyes
52 | Eminent empathy for the downhearted
56 | The unconditional love of royalty in disguise
59 | Keeping cool and calm is the sovereign way
62 | Humor rules the day

Marriage—Introduction

When Jennifer and her new boyfriend came home for the winter holidays in her freshmen year of college, her daddy and I received the surprise of our lives. Unbeknownst to our daughter, this young prince asked our permission to marry her.

I was hardly used to my nest being emptied for college, so perhaps many mothers could imagine my reaction to the idea of it being emptied forever. After all, with our daughter's departure for college came her return home for holidays and spring and summer breaks. Or at least that is the way I thought her college years were going to be.

But Jennifer chose a country boy for her prince—a country boy she had more or less known most of her life. This young man was four years older than she was, and was on track to go into the Air Force immediately following college. So while our daughter was just beginning her life away from home, he was in a mindset of setting up his own home and was ready for a wife to join him.

Long story short, we did not deny his request as long as Jennifer completed her college goals. Additionally, we did deny his first proposed wedding date, insisting they wait at least another year. This meant their wedding date was going to be a week before he had to report for duty in the Air Force. Our hope was that this would give them time to be certain that marriage to each other was what they wanted.

I don't know if it is possible for any twenty-year-old to know with whom they want to spend the rest of their life. But I attempted to be hopeful and trusted our daughter's judgment and respected her decision.

Their marriage lasted for five years, two deployments, and two Air Force bases. Its end is the next section in this book.

But for now and for her future consideration of marriage, I will write about my view of marriage as a love story—the kind of marriage I hope my princess will have someday.

I wanted to be the first in my family who didn't get a divorce. It looks like I've made it. Being married over thirty years has taught me much about the love that makes marriage go round and round.

I had heard that love often comes when you aren't looking for it. Such was true for me. Of course, often "love at first sight" is ignited by infatuation. But a spark can grow into a blazing fire when given proper attention. I believe marriage is a union of two hearts. Not a way of life, but life itself. I believe when husbands and wives live love, they give eternal life to their marriage.

In his definition of love in his letters to the Corinthians, Paul explains how to live love. He says that love is patient and kind. Love is not proud or self-seeking. Love is not easily angered and keeps no record of wrongs. Love always protects, trusts, hopes, and perseveres. Love never tires of loving.

With all my heart, I believe God is love. God is the source of love—kindness, compassion, and affection. Since husbands and wives are children of God, this makes them children of love. Both are unique and individual expressions of this love. This knowledge helped me pray through moments when I was tempted to see my husband (or myself) as anything but the expression of God's love.

I believe God has created us capable of expressing love. Understanding this has helped me see that I have the ability to choose and live love. With love as my center, it became natural to choose patience instead of frustration, empathy instead of criticism, joy instead of sadness, peace of mind instead of anger, trust instead of doubt, forgiveness instead of condemnation.

Of course, my conclusions today have been shaped by years of practice, progress, prayer, and many tender lessons.

In marriage, two people choose to share their lives with each other. Being together is effortless. Being together is so enjoyable you want time to stand still. Marriage is "being there" for each other. Taking care of each other. Making the other person feel special. Knowing what is needed without being asked. Communication in marriage is a sweet interchange of openness and respect. Giving each other encouragement is the greatest of all gifts.

Having fun together and laughing together is natural in marriage. Laughter keeps us from taking our own point of view too seriously. Laughter can break the spell of anger or frustration. In fact, laughter has helped me fulfill my grandmother's advice, "Never go to bed mad."

Romanic getaways and vacations nurture the love story—even if they last only moments. But they are moments for the husband and wife exclusively—walking in the park holding hands or having a candlelight dinner together. Or, if you live in the country like we do, having a rendezvous in a hay truck parked next to the stock pond surrounded by cows is pretty darn nice, too.

Marriage is strengthened by trust, enriched by passion, and brightened by sweet surprises. Remember this, dear daughter and daughters everywhere, and your marriage has a better chance of being a love story like I've been blessed to have with my prince. But even the most perfect love story includes some bumps and stumbles along the way. The essays ahead share many eye-openers I've learned during my married years.

Jealousy is the dragon

Early in my marriage, I often struggled with bouts of extreme sadness and anger as well as paranoia and fear. At the time, my husband and I had no idea I suffering from a bite by the "green-eyed monster." Jealousy is a nasty beast. Its wounds, if left undetected and untreated, can devastate a relationship.

I was yet to learn that jealousy was not the same as love. Sometimes people equate feeling jealous about someone with loving them. I'm here to tell you that jealousy is not love, but rather the fear of losing love.

Sadly, jealousy is all too familiar in human relationships. I suspect it crosses all cultures and ages. Jealousy is a topic of interest for scientists, songwriters, romance novelists, and theologians.

Of the human emotions, jealousy may be one of the most powerful and painful. It is deadly. Many times jealousy is noted as the motive for murder—today and in Biblical times. Jealousy seemed to be Cain's motivation for killing his brother, Abel (Genesis 4:1–8). It seemed to be what impelled Joseph's brothers to sell him into slavery (Genesis, chapter 37). It was probably part of the reason the Pharisees hated Jesus.

But must jealousy be normal, natural, and unavoidable?

I can say without a doubt, it is impossible to think clearly when you are jealous. Truth gets distorted, reason becomes clouded, and emotion turns irrational.

For me, jealousy could have been defined as the emotional reaction to a scenario in my mind that was not true. I often perceived situations and people as threats—even if it were family or friends. I thought if my husband spent time with them he must love them more than he loved me. I also had a deep fear of loss or betrayal, although this belief was completely unfounded. While I sensed my insecurities were without basis, I didn't know how to make a change.

Overcoming jealousy is like changing any emotional reaction or behavior. It begins with awareness.

In my search for help, I read Mary Baker Eddy's writings on marriage. The first statement that grabbed my attention was, "Jealousy is the grave of affection." She wrote of the "narrowness and jealousy" that seeks to confine a wife or a husband. She emphasized that home "should be the centre, though not the boundary, of the affections."

I eventually understood that living by the Golden Rule was imperative in marriage, as in all walks of life. As Jesus put it, "Whatsoever ye would that men should do to you, do ye even so to them" (Matthew 7:12). I wouldn't have liked my husband restricting the time I spent with my friends or family. I would not have liked being made to feel guilty about the time I did spend. But my husband was never the one who did these things—only me.

I knew my husband loved me and wanted me to be happy. He endeavored to do whatever he could to make me happy. He was a good friend to his many friends and a faithful and loving son to his parents. Should such admirable qualities and actions be punished by his wife?

So where did my unwarranted fear of losing his love come from? Perhaps these feelings came from being a child of divorced parents. In fact, everyone in my family had been married and divorced multiple times, so I didn't have any life examples of what a lasting, quality marriage looked like.

I also think I needed to become more aware of my spiritual identity as the woman God created—a whole-souled woman. Such a woman knows well the spiritual strength and fortitude her God endowed her with. She knows well how to live love, as Paul defined in 1 Corinthians, chapter 13. This love "cares more for others than for herself; doesn't want what it doesn't have; doesn't have a swelled head; isn't always 'me' first; doesn't keep score of the mistakes of others; doesn't revel when others grovel; always looks for the best; never looks back."

A woman with this kind of love has great patience and sees and appreciates goodness in everyone. Having a congenial temperament, she is not easily agitated. Her love is expansive enough to neutralize any friction. She is determined not to be offended when no wrong is meant.

The biggest thing that needed changing in my marriage was my view—mostly my view of myself. With my clarity came the recognition of and confidence in my husband's sincerity and love. My unfounded sadness, anger, paranoia, and fear were replaced with joy, satisfaction, peace of mind, and reassurance.

Divine Love gives all women the antidote for bites from the green-eyed monster. It is our whole-souled womanhood. It's something all daughters possess, but need to discover. Putting these qualities into practice in a marriage can heal jealousy wounds and build a permanent and powerful defense, enabling princesses to ward off any future approaches of this nasty beast. It sure worked for me!

Majestic communication and the Golden Rule

It's frustrating when one feels misunderstood. How can we be understood when we think no one is listening to what we're saying or our meaning is being misconstrued? In the essay, "Even kings can't read minds," I said there's an art to saying what we want to say. This "art" was not something I mastered quickly.

There were times early in my marriage when I felt like my husband and I were talking past each other. I knew that if we continued to talk past each other, agreements would never be reached, good decisions would never be made, and harmony and happiness would continue to elude us.

Empathy—the attempt to put oneself in another's shoes—is a worthy effort but not easy. I think this is especially difficult when the other person is your husband. Yet something told me that I must make a greater effort, or at least want to make an effort, if ever I hoped to have my husband do the same for me.

I began to realize that I was so busy thinking he wasn't listening to or understanding me that I wasn't listening to or caring about what he had to say. I was as guilty as I thought he was. What a vicious cycle talking past each other can be!

So what if I had to repeat myself from time to time or I had to rethink my word choice or use a different emphasis on select words to get my point across? I knew I had to do it. I must do whatever it took to understand and be understood. I wanted to understand my husband and wanted him to understand me, too. I wasn't going to give up on this goal.

I've heard that repetition impacts or improves our memory, but I'm not convinced mere repetition alone is what it takes for us to accomplish better understanding. No, I think it has much more to do with our sincere desire to listen and understand others. I think this kind of desire fuels the kind of effort that leads to mutual and accurate understanding.

When we are tempted to raise our voice to clarify our stance or we walk away in dismay or disappointment, we would be wise to rethink these actions. The louder I spoke, the more defensive or close-minded my husband became. I was guilty of walking away when feeling misunderstood. In fact, for a time, it was my most frequent response. But I finally realized the futility of such action. Of course there were times, when I felt angry for example, that walking away and cooling off before giving a response was a wise move.

I concluded that if I wanted to be understood better, I needed to make sure I was doing my best to understand. Communication, like any other aspect of our lives, is best served when we have the Golden Rule as our guide—yet again. This means listening and speaking to others (including husbands) in the way we long for them to listen and speak to us.

I remember when I was in Italy. I was impressed by the conversations I witnessed between Italian men and women. I was awed by the full attention they seemed to give each other. It was as if nothing else was going on around them but what was being said to one another.

I wanted my husband and me to talk with each other that way. I began to make a greater effort to listen to and understand his feelings, needs, and viewpoints.

Talking past each other eventually disappeared. It is so very wonderful to be able to have a sweet discussion of feelings, needs, and opinions. Whether or not we agree doesn't matter. But it is a powerful comfort to feel heard and understood. The better we have become in our mutual appreciation and understanding of one another's viewpoints, the more agreements we can reach.

I highly suggest that the newly married implement the Golden Rule in their communication if there are ever feelings of being misunderstood. It's the best guide for majestic communication with a king, queen, prince, princess, and everybody else, too.

When your prince surprises you, go with it

I love surprises—the pleasant kind! I can't get enough of them. This may in turn surprise my daughter, who probably thinks of me as the ultimate planner. It is true that I tend to always have a plan and a to-do list in hand. But what she may not realize is that I would also happily throw away a well-thought out plan for a nice surprise.

My husband surprised me one hot summer night. We were at a community outdoor concert and I longed to dance. But no one else was dancing. Suddenly, my sweet husband was standing in front of me offering his hand.

Did I take his hand? You bet I did! I delighted all the more in my dance with him because of the joy of surprise I was feeling.

Why was I surprised by his gesture? I wonder if my surprise had more to do with my low expectations than it did in his action. Of course, sometimes low expectations may be the result of a history of behavior in similar situations. I can recall attending many community dances where I didn't get his invitation to dance, which is perhaps why I wasn't expecting to dance with him that night.

I'm intrigued that my low expectations may have resulted in my surprise. The element of surprise seemed to make our dance all the more special.

I recall reading once upon a time that the citizens of Denmark had more life satisfaction than any other Western country. It was said that Denmark's secret was a culture of low expectations. In short, citizens of Denmark had low expectations each year and reported they were pleasantly surprised year after year when their year turned out better than expected.

While low expectations can become self-fulfilling prophecies, I understand the fear that high expectations may never be attained. No big dreams equals no big disappointment, some might say. Had I imposed my own expectations upon my husband and he failed to meet them, he would have failed to please me. Yet, I am surprised when he does something new because I didn't expect it.

I don't think the secret to satisfaction, especially in a marriage, is found in low expectations, but rather having the smallest expectations. We do expect fidelity, love, patience, strength. But by "smallest" I also mean humble, modest, simple, unpretentious, honest, and unpompous expectations for yourself and your husband. This would mean passing no judgment, making no assumptions or comparisons. There would be no reason to criticize, condemn, or complain. Nothing could offend or disappoint us.

We would move along in our marriage journey—learning, growing, loving, and living. We would recognize and respect our spouse as doing the same. We would be patient with ourselves and our mate as we strive to make progress ourselves.

Indeed, we can allow each day to surprise us with its discoveries and lessons. We can relish the joy of each surprising twist and turn of marriage. Our expectations can be for the joy of each surprise—especially when the surprise is a dance with our prince.

It's not all about tiaras and scepters

The American dream tells us it's possible to be whatever you imagine, to attain whatever you strive for, and to achieve your aspirations. Yes, anything is possible in the land of freedom and opportunity. The American dream defines the way success is gained—through hard work, determination, self-sacrifice, and perseverance.

Still for many, the "pot of gold" remains at the end of the rainbow—just out of reach. Do you ever wonder why this is? Perhaps it's because too many think success in the American dream is only measured by material wealth.

What if the American dream is not about a destination defined by fame and fortune? Could it be that a wrong definition of the American dream has led to destructive obsessions as well as a lack of satisfaction and happiness with one's life? To me, the American dream is about the journey—a journey of vision and hope that encourages creative initiative and inspires goal-making and the search for one's life purpose. Success is defined by a job well done and a good effort made.

In the early years of my marriage, my husband believed that the American dream was merely the quest for money. For years, he never thought we had enough. But how much is enough? His obsession with money became the impossible, never-to-be-reached dream telling him we needed more, we didn't have enough, we may never have enough, and we may run out.

I've seen the Biblical statement of the apostle Paul, "For the love of money is the root of all evil" misquoted as "Money is the root of all evil." But I don't think money in and of itself is the problem. I think Paul's words indicate it's our feelings about money that can lead to problems. I suspect it is our viewpoint about money that impacts how we answer the question, "How much is enough?"

In my newlywed years with my husband, we set a monetary goal we hoped to reach before our retirement. My husband always dreamed of retiring as early in life as possible.

The only problem with his plan was that as soon as we reached our savings goal, he increased the goal. We didn't have enough eggs in our basket—or so he said. In fact, I lost count of how many times our goal was increased.

I'm not so sure that economy and inflation were the main reasons he continually increased our nest egg. I finally told my husband that I didn't think we would ever have "enough." Or that he would never think we did.

Paul had it right. I think that a distorted perception of money is the root of many a problem and stress—and the cause of misinterpretations of the American dream. For my husband and me, this perception translated into worries about not having "enough" money for the rest of our lives. Not to be pessimistic, but who knows how long the rest of our lives will be?

I finally decided I didn't want to worry about money anymore. My husband and I were giving so much attention to our future that we kept ourselves from living more of our lives in the present.

Eventually, I was able to convince my husband that we needed to change the unsatisfying pattern into which we had boxed ourselves. I knew we needed to take to heart lessons I had learned from my mamma when I was growing up: Recognize all that we have. Be grateful for what we have. Enjoy what we have. I'm not just talking about money.

This attitude adjustment enabled us to focus more on the "now" moments of our life, to stop looking to the future to provide the answers, the opportunities, and the fulfilling of dreams; to improve today's moments, making the most of them; to consider present possibilities, right now; to no longer put off for tomorrow what could be done today, said today, or experienced today.

Having enough is not about having everything we want. Perhaps we have enough only as we appreciate and value what we already have.

Find beauty in the kingdom by opening your eyes

Mistaken impressions, rash judgments, believing the worst—I've done them all in my marriage and in other situations, too. Impressions of someone or something may be based on a stereotype, prejudice, or presumption and prove to be completely wrong.

The old adage, "You can't judge a book by its cover," is good advice. This means before we can judge, we need to take a deeper, closer look. Value and potential are not always obvious from what we see on the surface.

I learned such a lesson in the course of remodeling our house. We planned to replace several pieces of furniture that were worn out. I wanted our dining table to be one of them. But my husband wanted to refinish the table surface and have the chairs reupholstered. This was not my plan, but I compromised.

He worked hard and diligently on the table, and when he had completed his work, my first impression was not good. In fact, my initial reaction was honestly, "I hate it." But I resolved that I was stuck with it—at least for a while.

Then something unexpected and interesting happened. Various friends and family members—including my daughter—saw our refinished dining table, and they all loved it. I couldn't believe it! Not one saw my point of view. Eventually, I began to wonder if I had unfairly judged. As I began to give the table another look, my opinion shifted from dislike to love. Yes, I reached a point where I truly loved the refinished results.

How could this have happened? Had the table's appearance changed? Hardly! So, what was different?

I think my disappointment in not purchasing a new dining table created the unconscious presumption that I would not like the refinished table. I didn't want to like it. My mind had been made up before the refinishing even began. I had been fooled by my point of view.

I began to understand how my impressions influence my judgments.

What if our impression of the human scene is a difficult and frightening picture of a loved one in a hospital bed? We can become convinced that the evidence before our eyes tells the true, whole story and believe the worst.

I'm remembering several years ago when my stepdad was in the hospital. He was in a medically induced coma for several weeks. This had followed complications from heart bypass surgery. It was alarming and disheartening to see him this way. At times my mamma and I thought he was dead and was just being kept alive by the various machines. Indeed, his physicians were concerned and uncertain of his recovery.

One of our prayers became not to be fooled by the view. Before entering his room, we would fill our thoughts with what we believed Mother Love sees—one of her beloved children, spiritual, perfect, whole, full of vitality and strength.

Weeks later, after much progress, the induced coma was discontinued and my stepdad awoke with a smile as his good-humored, natural self. More progress would be needed, but he did recover. The one-time view of the near-death scenario was indeed proven false.

I've thought about this experience many times when faced with illness myself. Along with my prayers is a protest against the view that includes a picture of disease and its symptoms, pain, and so forth. I turn my thought to what I believe Divine Love's view of me is as her child, created in her image and likeness. There's reassurance, expectation, and healing in this approach. I've also found this approach helpful when faced with a stubborn prince, or when I was angry or frustrated by something my prince did or didn't do.

I've learned that anything that would rob me of my hope, joy, or peace of mind must be warded off. I must not allow any view to tempt me into believing that the human picture of problems and struggles is the end of the story.

A good beginning is to not be fooled into thinking our point of view is the only one. Our opinion might change when we aren't so quick to jump to conclusions and believe our assumptions, our first impressions, or even our worst fears. Open your eyes to see the beauty in the kingdom all around you.

Eminent empathy for the downhearted

Maybe you know the fellow—his lordship for whom nothing is ever right. It's too hot, it's too cold, his boss is a jerk, the food is lousy—he has a gripe for every situation. He's never happy. He looks for fault and finds it. He points fingers and blames everyone and everything—except himself, of course. He offers no solutions because he can't see any. He's the friend or family member you would most like to avoid because his ill temper can quickly turn a joy-filled room into a negative and pessimistic atmosphere.

If you're on the receiving end of his many complaints, consider this: The complainer in your life really doesn't want to argue. However, ignoring him will only make him grumble and growl louder and longer. Your complainer actually yearns to be understood. He has a need to have his concerns and frustrations acknowledged. There's only one thing that may begin to quiet his clamoring—an empathetic response. My husband hasn't been as bad as the fellow I've described, but he has struggled with his own long list of complaints. So have I.

Empathy is not the same as sympathy for the complainer. Empathy is not apathy that doesn't care how the grumbler feels, or sheer disagreement with the complainer's outcries. Rather, empathy is putting yourself in the grumbler's shoes (the best you can) and sincerely trying to understand his feelings.

How in the world is it possible to put yourself in your husband's shoes when you're struggling even to understand his point of view?

In order to do this, I had to look beyond or beneath my husband's complaints. I found a heap of worry, fear, depression, and discouragement. These emotions frequently resulted in a barrage of grievances that masked the basis for his woes. Perhaps the protests were an unconscious way to get my attention. Or perhaps it was his attempt to do something—anything—because he didn't know what else to do to improve his situation, since he was so consumed with his worries and discouragement.

One time, my husband's discouragement reminded me of a story that I had read and heard in various forms many times. I shared this story with him. Apparently the Devil had an array of tools attractively displayed and priced—envy, jealousy, hatred, and pride, among many others. Then, off in a corner by itself was a harmless-looking, wedge-shaped, well-worn tool that had a higher price than any of the others. Someone asked the Devil what this tool was, and he answered, "That's discouragement." When he was asked why it cost more than all the others, he boasted, "With this tool I can get into a man's heart and mind and do just about anything I want."

The Devil knew that nothing could paralyze, stop, or control us more than discouragement. Discouragement can keep the unemployed unemployed; the homeless homeless; the sick sick; and the complainer complaining. Discouragement drains us of courage, vision, faith, and expectation.

In one version of the story, someone asked the Devil if the tool worked on everyone. The Devil reluctantly answered, "No, it doesn't work on a person with a grateful heart."

I heard this version at a time in my marriage when my poor husband was complaining about this and then that. (I was, too, actually.) The idea of feeling grateful was difficult for him because he felt nothing was going his way. His bitterness, discontentment, and discouragement were more than he could bear. He longed for solutions, but the idea of a grateful heart seemed unreachable for him.

One day during his Bible study time, he told me that he came across three verses in the first epistle of Paul to the Thessalonians that appeared to hold the secret to cultivating a grateful heart: "Always be joyful. Never stop praying. Be thankful in all circumstances" (1 Thessalonians 5:16–18).

My sweet husband began thanking God with all his heart for any and all good in his life, whether seen in small or big ways. Moment-by-moment prayer was indeed required, but his prayers were not petitions to God. Instead, they were affirmations of God's presence and power. These affirmations also became declarations and promises to not allow any circumstance to take his joy from him—something he learned from my mamma, too. His discouraged heart was soon replaced with a grateful heart filled with encouragement. His reasons for complaining diminished till they disappeared.

My husband discovered that as we acknowledge Divine Love's goodness in our lives, we can begin to believe Love has a perfect plan and purpose for us. Our eyes are opened to the good that is always at hand, and gratitude keeps us expectant of more good.

If any of you princesses are faced with a complainer in your life, try a little empathy. If you're ever feeling overwhelmed with complaints yourself, take it from an experienced complainer—cultivating a grateful heart is your best bet for an improved outlook and better future. Don't let discouragement take you down!

The unconditional love of royalty in disguise

It had been a really bad day. I was caught up in a range of emotions from betrayal and hurt to disappointment and anger. Once again, my father-in-law had been rude and arrogant with me, bringing me to tears, and my husband just stood by and did nothing. Once again, I said things that I wished I hadn't.

For the record, this behavior pattern improved in time with lots of patience, love, and forgiveness on my part. My husband eventually gained more courage and confidence in standing up to his dad. My father-in-law's disposition completely changed from tyrant to teddy bear.

But this particular day, my dismay and anguish might have been beyond relief if it had not been for the happy yelp and wagging tail of my little Lady dachshund that met me as I walked through my door.

After spending a couple of hours holding my puppy in my lap and being lavished with extravagant licks, I suddenly realized that my world didn't seem so terribly wronged. My peace of mind, which hours earlier seemed forever disturbed, was returning. I could feel a calmness taking over that was allowing me to once again think rationally and clearly.

I've heard that dogs truly are man's best friends because they can directly promote our wellbeing by buffering us from stress. I've even heard dog owners have fewer medical problems than those who aren't. If there is a serious illness, dog owners tend to recover more quickly. I certainly feel much better after I spend quality time with my doxey!

I always feel an unconditional love and unquestionable loyalty when I'm in her presence. She appears unconscious of my faults, failures, or weaknesses. Thank goodness! Her faithfulness is never fleeting—it has no strings attached. Her love continues day after day and is freely given.

As I sat there cherishing the moments spent with my dachshund, I thought to myself: "Who else but this little dog loves me unconditionally?" In that moment as I basked in the love of my dog, I remembered there is another who loves me like this—God.

It's really no surprise that God loves us all—including my father-in-law and husband—constantly, faithfully, and without conditions, since God is love. There's a parable Jesus shares that for me epitomizes God as love while teaching lessons about what it means to love and be loved. It's the story about the prodigal son (Luke 15:11–32). Many are familiar with the younger son, who leaves home. But there is another son in that story I don't always remember. The parable begins, in fact, "There was once a man who had two sons."

The younger of the two sons asked his daddy to give him his inheritance early because he wanted to leave home to go out on his own. But this younger son didn't make wise decisions and eventually wasted all of his money. It wasn't until he was starving and slopping pigs for his living that he decided to go home and ask his daddy if he would hire him, since he no longer felt worthy of being treated as a son. At least his daddy fed his hired servants three meals a day!

But when the father saw this young son whom he had given up for dead, he felt only love. This father saw no faults, failures, or weaknesses in his son. He saw only a much beloved son whom he wanted to embrace.

All the years since the younger son left, the older son had remained ever faithful and diligent in service to his dad. Now this older son felt unappreciated as he watched his dad celebrating his brother's return after he had wasted everything their dad had given to him.

But again, this patient and compassionate father reminded the older son of his appreciation for his faithfulness. The father said, "Everything that is mine is yours." He also told his older son that it was right to celebrate the safe return of his younger brother.

Because that is what Love does—Love loves.

As I thought about God's love for me, I knew Mother Love was giving no concern to the faults, failures, and weaknesses that were mine—or those of others. She was too busy loving me and everyone to see anything less than her beloved children.

I thought, *Perhaps I need to do the same. Maybe I can forgive and forget what I consider someone else's faults and failures (like those of my father-in-law and husband). I can do this because I love them.* I also realized that I could forgive and forget what I was considering my fault and failure in the situation (losing my temper and perhaps even over-reacting) because I needed to love myself in the way that Divine Love loves me.

Interestingly enough, as I sat there feeling quite loved by my dog and very loved by God, it was not long before I could feel nothing else but love. What was a very bad day was transformed into a doggone good one.

Keeping cool and calm is the sovereign way

I like to think of myself as a recovering over-reactor. I do fall off my throne from time to time, as my daughter could testify, but I do my best to keep my reactions in check.

I woke up one particular morning in a state of exasperation. My week had been a busy one, filled to the brim with appointments, meetings, and unfinished tasks. Never mind that I created and even desired most of the activities on my agenda. I couldn't get past the irrational feelings of irritation that I didn't have enough time to do all that I thought I had to do.

So the fact that I was running late to my hair appointment and leaving my dirty house and piled laundry behind was more than I could handle. That the car in front of me was going at least twenty miles below the speed limit didn't help matters either.

I ranted and raved most of the way to the beauty shop. Fortunately, I wasn't alone with my inconsequential and insignificant ranting. My dear daughter was home from college and soon became my needed voice of reason.

As she sat there in the car listening to me, she calmly pointed out that everything I was stressing over was easily fixable and could be corrected—maybe not all that very day, mind you, but it was all doable nonetheless.

She emphasized that my getting all worked up was blowing everything out of proportion and was not going to help me accomplish what I needed and wanted. She was right, of course. I knew this. But the "drama queen" in me needed to be reminded.

Making a mountain out of molehill only results in one thing—a big deal being made out of something minor. Whenever I made "mountains," I made things more difficult than they had to be.

I recall hearing someone say once, "Don't sweat the small stuff when so much else matters." It turned out that most of what was making me sweat was all very small when proper perspective took over my sanity. I began to ask myself, *Will I remember a year from now what is driving me crazy today? Can I remember which days last year I was late for my hair appointments? Or which days my house was dirty or which days I got behind on laundry?* Of course I couldn't! Why couldn't I? Because those things are small stuff in comparison with the grander things that make up my life and my treasured memories.

I do try very hard not to waste time getting upset over things—especially things my husband does or doesn't do that annoy me—that weigh not one iota among the things that do matter most to me. I can promise you that the only thing that overreacting achieves is wasted time and needless misery.

I have found comfort in remembering the words of Jesus, "Let not your heart be troubled" (John 14:27) and the Psalmist, "Fret not thyself" (Psalms 37:7). These words of wisdom usually help redirect my focus and help calm my irrational emotions.

I remember when Jesus calmed the storm at sea, saying, "Peace, be still" (Mark 4:39). His healing declaration can also calm what seems like a storm brewing in my weary mind. I can then find my center again—no longer caught up in the minutiae of a frantic moment.

My precious princess was right. Life can have enough drama in it at times without us adding more to it. Besides—sweating too much over the small stuff will keep us from experiencing and enjoying what is important to us.

I thank my princess for being my voice of reason that day and many other days since.

Humor rules the day

What a way to start the day!

I was dreaming one of the most absurd dreams I've ever dreamed. I can't remember now what it was about. I only remember that I began snickering. Then, I began giggling at the fact that I was snickering—in my sleep.

My giggles were soon followed by my husband's chuckles. When he finally asked me what was so funny, my giggles turned into belly laughs. My husband and I hee-hawed until the bed shook with our amusement.

I was reminded of the famous phrase, "Laugh and the world laughs with you." My husband started laughing with me even though he had no idea why I was laughing.

Interestingly enough, I couldn't stop smiling throughout my day. Every so often, I would recall my laughter-filled morning and I'd start chuckling again. I must say that it was one of the most delightful days I've ever had. I found humor in everything.

I don't think anything feels better than a good burst of laughter.

It occurs to me now that perhaps this is a good way to approach many things in life.

I've read about the health benefits of humor and laughter. Besides the list of physical benefits frequently given, the ability to find humor in our life experiences—even in extremes—can help us look at our problems in a fresh way. Plus, seeing the humor in some of our most difficult scenarios can help to normalize our experience, particularly by keeping things from appearing too overwhelming.

Think about some of the everyday life situations often portrayed in comedy sitcoms. It's usually when everything goes wrong time and again when we laugh the most. Are we able to laugh at ourselves on those days when everything seems to go wrong? Maybe we should.

It could be that our ability to find the humor in our lives is a powerful aid to finding solutions, making progress, and ultimately overcoming whatever it is that would bring us down or hold us back.

At the very least, we might be happier and more energized as we go about our day.

I had a childhood friend who never failed to see the humor in everything. In fact, my mamma sometimes denied my requests to have this friend sleep over because she laughed so much. Mamma said she could hear us laughing all night and consequently didn't get much sleep.

Mamma was right about one thing. My friend laughed all the time. She made me laugh, too. She taught me lessons about finding humor in things that I've never forgotten. I can honestly say she was the happiest person I've ever known. I wanted to be like her and I still do.

I think the ability to laugh at ourselves keeps us from taking ourselves too seriously and helps keep our egos in check. There have been many times when I've gotten angry at my husband.

After my outburst—when we've stood there looking at each other in a standoff of wills—we've often begun laughing. I think one of the times people look the most ridiculous is when they are angry.

The wonder and power of those moments, when our anger was followed by laughter, is that whatever prompted the anger in the first place became a smaller issue than it at first seemed. My husband and I could then make any adjustments that we both felt were reasonable.

Waking up laughing is a better way to start the day than getting up on the wrong side of the bed. Even when I don't wake up laughing, I plan to do my best to find the humor in everything each day. My husband and I have proven that this approach keeps problems solvable and life happier and more satisfying.

Part Three
Divorce and other drama

67 | Introduction
69 | Be kind to your first subject—yourself
72 | Banish Debbie Downer from the realm
75 | Replace panic with queenly poise
79 | Nobility knows its own worth
82 | When in doubt, consult the royal Mouse
86 | Princesses rise and shine—never rise and whine
89 | A princess's worst enemy or best ally—herself
92 | A royal decree: follow your dreams
95 | Rulers look ahead, not behind
98 | Never doubt your greatness
101 | A queen asks, "Why not?"
104 | Even in a castle, some days are like that
107 | Happiness comes with the territory

Divorce and other drama — Introduction

Even world-famous princesses don't always stay married to their prince. After seven years with an empty nest, John and I had learned to relish our privacy. We were enjoying excursions together, and life was good. What we didn't see coming or expect was a phone call from our daughter saying she was on the way home.

Jennifer had been married for five years. She and her husband had bought their first house in Shreveport, Louisiana, about a mile from Barksdale Air Force Base where her husband was stationed. She had recently completed what was to be her first master's degree, but she had not been able to find a job yet in her career field of interest—teaching college literature. We thought she was happy. Apparently, we were wrong.

It seems Jennifer's unrest in her marriage was compounded following the death of a good friend and fellow soldier friend to her husband. Her new view of life and death led her to look at her own life and goals in a more urgent way. Her eventual conclusion prompted her to leave her husband. Life suddenly looked much shorter to her, and I think perhaps she realized she was not being honest about her feelings—to herself or to her husband. In short, she hadn't known whom she wanted to be married to for the rest of her life when she was twenty years old.

For the next year, Jennifer and her dachshund Bella lived at home with us while she completed the divorce process, prayed, and explored diligently to find new goals for herself. This journey eventually placed her back in college to get another master's degree, this time in history. She decided she wanted to teach college history instead of college English.

With that master's degree complete, Jennifer will soon have her Ph.D. in history and be on her way to fulfilling her career dreams. Her new prince happens to share her dreams—to teach college history. She lives in her own house and is happier and more satisfied with her life and goals than I've ever seen her.

Starting over is not always the easy road to take. My mamma divorced my daddy after twenty-six years of marriage, and it turned out to be the right thing to do. We must follow our heart and be honest and true with ourselves. We need to have the courage to act when we feel we must. There will be an open door when one door closes. Often it takes walking out the first door to see the other open door waiting for us.

The essays that follow try to offer encouragement and hope if you find yourself facing any type of dramatic difficulty or unexpected change.

Be kind to your first subject—yourself

The Bible often speaks of Jesus as being "moved with compassion." His compassion was soon followed by his healing the sick and feeding the hungry. He even taught about the need for compassion in many of the parables and stories he told to his followers. In fact, compassion is considered by the major religious traditions as among the greatest of virtues.

More than empathy, compassion is defined as the feeling that gives rise to an active desire to alleviate another's suffering. Mercy and tenderness are among its synonyms, while cruelty and indifference are its opposite.

I sometimes wonder what a little compassion could do for our troubled and weary world—in negotiations, interrogations, debates, and discussions. As we see the suffering of others and our hearts ache for their pain, do we wish we could help in some way? Making a difference in someone's life does not necessarily require lots of money or time.

The compassionate understanding and kindness shown to me when I have failed or made mistakes encouraged my growth and eventual successes. Our words can have a powerful impact on friend or foe.

It was the note from a college counselor when I was home on academic suspension that gave me the encouragement to believe I could improve my study skills and be successful in college. I returned to my beloved school a few months later after attending a local community college for a semester (where I made the Dean's List). Three years later I completed my bachelor's degree and received the graduating class award for "general progress."

It's helpful to remember that we are all in the same boat sharing this human experience. We are never alone. Others have undoubtedly walked in our shoes before. We're not the only ones who have made the very same mistake or used bad judgment.

Have you found it easy to show compassion toward a friend or family member—or even a stranger—who's having a tough time, but you get angry or frustrated with yourself when your own life falls short of your ideals?

Perhaps you need a big dose of self-compassion. This is something I told my daughter as she anguished over her divorce.

Things will not always go the way we want them to. We need to learn to give the same comfort and care to ourselves that we would give to others. Showing compassion and understanding when confronted with personal failings will help us put our mistakes into a larger life perspective—a more balanced, objective point of view—and encourage our progress.

But let's be clear about what self-compassion is not.

Self-compassion is not self-pity. It serves no good purpose to get lost in our emotional drama or immerse ourselves into a problem.

Self-compassion is not self-indulgence. There is nothing beneficial about indulging in unhealthy rewards or habits.

Self-compassion is not self-condemnation. Judging and criticizing ourselves for inadequacies or shortcomings keeps our attention and focus on the negative or buried in the past.

With compassion for ourselves when we have missteps, we inspire and prompt wiser steps that move us forward and closer to reaching our potential. We are better equipped and able to keep a clear eye on our goals.

A baby learning to walk doesn't think twice about trying again after she falls down. That baby will likely fall many times before she masters walking. But she doesn't stop with walking. After she learns to walk, she tries running, then skipping, and then jumping. Before walking, she scooted, crawled, and probably even climbed.

The idea is that we keep moving, learning, progressing, and mastering new skills, and gaining new insights and knowledge along the way. Yes, you may fall sometimes. It may take you a while to get where you want to go. But never stop trying.

Compassion will keep you moving forward. Give yourself a hug when you need one. Pat yourself on the back and say everything will be okay. Be like the baby who doesn't think twice about her fall. Be the princess who in the end gains her crown.

Banish Debbie Downer from the realm

There seems to be one in every kingdom—the naysayer, the voice of doom, the predictor of bad tidings. Debbie Downer or Gloomy Gus is always the pessimist who sees the downside of everything—the glass that is always half empty. She or he generally shares a depressed view of the world with everyone they meet. My husband John can sometimes be a Gloomy Gus. I told my daughter she isn't the only princess who has ever struggled with a Debbie Downer complex.

Perhaps among the disciples of Jesus, the unbelieving Thomas would come under the same or at least a similar category. Skeptics seem to have little or no faith in what they haven't seen or experienced. Their dark perspective would have us all believe the possible is impossible unless they are proven wrong. Even when proven wrong, they consider it a fluke, a stroke of good luck, a chance occurrence, an accident.

Of course, Thomas did eventually believe, and his faith was restored. But his doubting brought a lesson from Jesus. Jesus said, "Thomas, because thou hast seen me, thou hast believed: blessed are they that have not seen, and yet have believed" (John 20:29).

Perhaps a lack of faith or not enough faith is the culprit that leads to pessimism.

I'm no Little Mary Sunshine, but most of the time I just can't subscribe to Debbie Downer's view on life. I have firsthand experience in how a simple change in my outlook and attitude changes my experience for better or for worse. Who wouldn't want to do whatever it takes to have a better, happier, more satisfying life?

One problem I see with Debbie and Gus is that they are too opinionated. In fact, they are so consumed by their own opinions that their minds are completely closed to divine direction, inspiration, and intervention—even when they say they have faith in God.

During her divorce and search for new goals, my daughter gained much inspiration from the parable of the drowning man. It has a variety of versions, but one story says a man's house is being immersed by a flood. Before the road is covered, someone in a jeep drives by and offers the man a ride. But the man refuses, saying he has faith that God will save him. As the waters continue to rise, another comes by in a boat and offers the man a ride. Again, the man refuses, saying he has faith that God will save him. Finally, while the man is standing on his rooftop, a helicopter arrives and the pilot offers the man a ride to safety. Yet again, the man refuses, expressing his faith in God. In heaven, the man asks why God didn't save him. The Divine Parent explains, "I sent you a jeep, a boat, and a helicopter."

Have you ever been like this man and tried to interfere with or limit how God's purpose would work out? I've learned that there are infinite resources and possibilities—that nothing is impossible or beyond reach. He could have accepted the jeep ride, I told my daughter—without question, judgment, or fear.

I prefer to believe Love's plan for us is always good, and I'd rather trust in her wisdom than uncertain opinion or fearful odds. Don't become a Debbie Downer and let your hope be diminished or your confidence overshadowed by doom and gloom. Interrupt Debbie's pouting with some cheer, and you may just find the encouragement that brightens your spirits.

So what if you're like the drowning man and you refused the jeep and boat ride? Would you sit there, like I suspect Debbie or Gus would, on your rooftop with your head down on your knees—dismayed and depressed—condemning yourself for your mistakes, your lack of wisdom, your arrogance?

Since that perspective would never save my daughter or anyone else, here's a more reliable plan of action. You can't drive forward staring in the rearview mirror. Actions or inactions in the past are history. Move on. It's not too late to start over, to make new goals, to dream new dreams or go after old ones. Keep your chin up, your hope high, your view expectant. Keep your eyes peeled for a helicopter—that new idea that will take you where you want to go. Be ready to take it!

My "helicopter" idea was a decision to quit a job after eight years and start down a new career path. I wanted to be a newspaper columnist. After my first essay was published in the *Dallas Morning News,* other area newspapers asked me to share my columns with them. Eventually, I had a weekly column that was being published in numerous Texas newspapers as well as parenting magazines and a variety of websites, too.

So go back to school if you're so inclined. Change your major. Explore new hobbies. Goals will become clear as you move forward. You just have to move and keep on moving!

Replace panic with queenly poise

Perhaps we've all had days when panic directed our actions or we were disheartened because we saw no solution in sight. At such times it can be difficult to know who to trust for answers.

I think a preoccupation with fear and worry has often incited my panic.

Prayer and meditation enables me to feel Divine Love's presence and realize that I am enveloped in her love. There is power in acknowledging her presence.

I have suffered many times from panic attacks. When faced with conflict, dilemmas, or any turmoil—whether real or perceived—I've often become a physical and emotional wreck. So I can testify that when the going gets tough, leaning on God is better than panic.

Remembering your queenly poise and taking some deep spiritual breaths in times of crisis, pressure, and immense stress can enable us to be comforted and reassured by God's ever-presence. Panic will be replaced by peace, and peace quiets fear and calms anxiety. We can reach a state of mind that fosters inspiration and revelation. Then, we will be able to see solutions realized and implemented. Problems that at first seem huge or beyond repair can become small (or much smaller) and fixable.

"Thou wilt keep him in perfect peace, whose mind is stayed on thee" (Isaiah 26:3). I love this promise!

The Psalmist wrote, "Yea, though I walk through the valley of the shadow of death, I will fear no evil: for thou art with me" (Psalms 23:4). It could be said that the "valley" represents any difficult or terrifying experience we face. "For thou art with me" is a promise that usually dissipates my fear. That the Lord makes us strong when we are weak is another promise I cling to often.

There was a year when I felt like I was getting hit with one catastrophe after another. My father-in-law lost his battle with cancer. My oldest brother was in the hospital receiving long-term care. I became consumed with fears of cancer myself and had thyroid surgery and a hysterectomy which had been preceded by severe menopausal symptoms. Then another brother overdosed on prescription drugs and ended up in the hospital with my oldest brother. My mamma fell several times, but thankfully never broke any bones. I was in a constant state of waiting for the next shoe to drop. One night, the pressure in my chest increased until I could not even lie down and breathe normally. I felt like I was going to explode.

In my anguish, I prayed. I began with the Lord's Prayer. As my uneasy thoughts began to calm, I let go of the internal struggle. I put aside all the details weighing on my heart. I stopped my mind from hurrying to tomorrow or next week or next year. I focused only on feeling God's presence.

"The Lord will bless his people with peace" (Psalms 29:11). I felt blessed with peace. My weary night turned into restful breaths and sleep. The next morning, I awoke refreshed and still confident of God's ever-presence. The discomfort in my chest dissipated, never to return.

A few months later, in spite of worries that the day would never come, my oldest brother did get well enough to return home. The brother who overdosed recovered, promising to never do that again—and he has kept his word.

My fears of cancer required many hours in quiet contemplation talking with God the way my mamma taught me. But it came down to one reassuring fact—what became a fact to me, anyway—that God loved me and was always with me.

Moment by moment, I had to embrace—completely inhale actually—the feeling that God is Love and that she loved me, that God is good and surely she wanted only good for her children. No matter where I was, what I did, what decisions I made—no matter what—God was with me and loved me. Pondering this kept me from losing all hope no matter what health issue or fear I faced.

I asked myself these questions: Can I ever be somewhere where God isn't? Is there ever a moment when God doesn't care about me? Can anyone or anything have more control over my life than God?

I really love Psalms 139:7-10: "If I make my bed in hell" or "dwell in the uttermost parts of the sea"—"even there" it says—God's love and presence is with me.

After many months, including two successful surgeries and recovery with benign results on all biopsies, a more certain sense of God's love and presence became more dominant in my thought than morbid fears. Actually this more certain sense came before my surgeries. I felt it right before I went into the first one and have kept it ever since.

So now, I bathe myself daily in God's love. I want to feel God's love and presence, relish in it, breathe it in, ponder it, and rest in that knowledge. I concluded that God summons us to live. That's what we must do.

Stay grounded in your spirituality, dear daughters. Rest your thoughts on the spiritual rock, which you can think of as spiritual knowledge, which affirms God's presence, omnipotence, and goodness. Then you'll be like that wise man in Jesus' parable who built his house upon a rock. "And the rain descended, and the floods came, and the winds blew, and beat upon that house; and it fell not: for it was founded upon a rock" (Matthew 7:24–25).

Panic paralyzes, cripples, blinds, and stifles. From my own experience I've concluded that panic is a reaction—an unconscious choice—that serves no good purpose and isn't helpful or productive.

As I've told my darling princess, when your first instinct is to panic, you can consciously choose to pray. Prayer can reassure and remind you that anything is possible, that possibilities are infinite, and that God is with you. Prayer can enable you to move forward, reach new heights, overcome hurdles, and break new ground.

There is no good time to panic. With queenly poise and prayer you will persevere!

Nobility knows its own worth

The following questions are directed to all daughters out there:
- Did you ever not apply for the job you wanted because you thought you wouldn't get it anyway?
- Do you feel it's too late to start a new career, so you continue on your current path even though you're miserable?
- Have you settled for a relationship with someone because you believe this is as good as it can get for you?
- When someone pays you a compliment, is your first response to deny and discount rather than simply saying thanks?

If you can answer "yes" to any of these questions, then you may be suffering from a bad case of self-doubt. It's time to grab your pompoms and give yourself a cheer.

Have you ever seen the YouTube video titled, "Jessica's Daily Affirmation"? An adorable, precocious little girl stands on her bathroom counter at the mirror proclaiming all that is wonderful about what she sees and declaring her grand expectations for her day and life.

It seems children are born with an innate sense of appreciation for themselves. I remember those days. I sometimes wonder what happened to my ability to cheer for myself and my life in a positive and passionate way.

Somewhere along our life journey, I think we learn to argue with and against ourselves. In doing so, we lost the high regard we once had and became obsessed with self-criticism.

The good news is we can learn to root for ourselves again and stop underestimating our potential and settling for less than our best.

Self-appreciation is not arrogance. There is nothing wrong with valuing and honoring our God-given gifts, talents, abilities, and skills. I have no doubt that Mother Love cherishes and blesses the uniqueness of each of her precious children. Why would we not do the same?

Of course we should celebrate our successes! Why should we only have pity-parties?

You are not inadequate, insufficient, deficient, limited in any way. You are not at a disadvantage. When you make an estimate of the quality or worth of yourself or your abilities that is lower than what Love makes, you are cheating yourself out of seeing your potential, genius, passion, and purpose. You need to recognize your value in order to reach it.

You have only become unmindful or forgetful of the child God created. This child—like little Jessica—knows very well that anything is possible and whatever is possible will be great.

To me, Jessica's daily affirmations are a good way to begin each day. We can make daily affirmations of our strengths and capabilities when we wake up each morning. It makes sense that if we are to reach our full potential, we need to begin by appreciating who we are and what we can do.

I tried this a few years back when I was desperate to lose some weight—thirty pounds to be exact. I was consumed with discouragement—so much so, that I didn't know where to begin to get rid of the unwanted pounds. After watching Jessica's video, I realized I wasn't exactly on my own sidelines cheering myself on. I began to give myself a pep talk before I got out of bed every morning. Then I was fired up to take what became my daily morning walk. Sometimes I had to give myself additional pep talks throughout the day, especially when I was tempted to overindulge with desserts. My diet was more about discipline and control than depriving myself. The amazing thing was that this pattern of discipline, routine, and cheerleading helped me reach my goal in just a few months.

So be your own ally, friend, cheerleader. Know you can count on yourself to be in your own corner every step of your life journey. Know that God is right there alongside of you cheering, applauding, and rooting for her child with you.

Today is big with prospects, possibilities, and potential. Tomorrow promises to be even brighter. Your enthusiasm and exuberance for each day will give you the sparkle, hope, faith, inspiration, and encouragement you need to make each day all that it can be.

Princesses and future queens, you've got a lot in your favor. Never sell yourself short!

When in doubt, consult the royal Mouse

I was excited to learn that the Dallas Symphony was paying tribute to Disney music, and I couldn't wait to take my mamma and my daughter with me. Clips of beloved Disney movies were going to be shown on a big screen while the symphony played the coordinating soundtracks. This would mean I'd get a glimpse of Mickey. This was shortly after my daughter came home while she went through divorce proceedings, and I had hoped to bring her some cheer and hope. Mickey has always had this effect on me.

I wasn't disappointed. As the lights dimmed, his smiling face with those adorable ears appeared before me. I didn't need to hear the words when the music began—I knew them all too well. My eyes swelled with tears, as I quietly sang along, "Who's the leader of the club that's made for you and me? M-I-C-K-E-Y M-O-U-S-E!"

Symphony rule number one: No singing along with the music, my daughter reminded me.

Were they kidding me? There was no way I could sit there and not sing my song! After all, I was born a "Mouseketeer," named after Annette Funicello. It's difficult to find the words to express the depth of my emotion every time I see the Mouse.

What is it about Mickey?

Walt Disney once said, "Mickey Mouse is, to me, a symbol of independence. He was a means to an end. He popped out of my mind onto a drawing pad...on a train ride from Manhattan to Hollywood at a time when business fortunes of my brother Roy and myself were at lowest ebb and disaster seemed right around the corner."

Mickey Mouse may have given Walt Disney and his brother the financial independence they sought, but Mickey has always given me hope.

I loved learning about Mickey's history as it seemed the very essence of hope. I knew his story could fill my daughter with hope, too. It's a story that illustrates the darkest part of day before the dawn. Hope assures us that there is always a way out of darkness—that dawn always comes.

A new day, new possibilities, new discoveries, new opportunities, new ideas—Mickey Mouse provided all of this for Walt and Roy Disney. When I'm in Mickey's presence, I'm reminded all of these are available to me, too.

My daughter was raised watching Disney movies, so I know she remembers very well that every Disney story portrays "evil" trying to destroy "good," and that by each story's end, "evil" fails. Disney stories provide a message of hope to anyone who has doubt about which is the stronger—good or evil.

I also believe the words of Paul in the Bible empower us when we are faced with challenges that would overwhelm and bring us down. He says, "Be not overcome of evil, but overcome evil with good" (Romans 12:21). This sums up, to me, every Disney story climax—the character representing good proves that evil will not have the final say.

I believe we claim our spiritual heritage as children of a loving God by looking for good, expecting it and having confidence in it. There is not a power stronger or greater than God. We have the God-given ability and capability to overcome the myriad forms of evil with good—with the power of God's promise of good. We have this divine assurance, "For I know the thoughts that I think toward you, saith the Lord, thoughts of peace, and not of evil, to give you an expected end" (Jeremiah 29:9).

So in any dark times in her life, I tell my daughter that her hope can't be forever dimmed, diminished, or destroyed. It may feel like the dawn is never going to arrive, but rest assured it will. God's promise of good can't be stopped from coming forth. The Bible instructs, "Cast not away therefore your confidence, which hath great recompence of reward" (Hebrews 10:35). Indeed, God promises you an "expected end"—the recovery you are anticipating, the plan you are looking forward to, the improvement you are counting on.

We can know, "Every good gift and every perfect gift is from above, and cometh down from the Father of lights, with whom is no variableness, neither shadow of turning" (James 1:17). We can trust in this truth, and, as Jesus promised, "And ye shall know the truth, and the truth shall make you free" (John 8:32). Trusting in God's truths—her laws, her assurances, her promises—will enable us all to discover the solutions and answers we long for.

The concert was about to end, and my daughter whispered that we had to go home and watch a Disney movie. "Good idea," I said.

And once again, I couldn't help but sing the last verse of my song: "M-I-C—see ya real soon! K-E-Y—Why? Because we like you. M-O-U-S-E."

After we got home and watched our movie and everything was suddenly brighter in my princess's eyes, I reminded her to always remember: When you need a good dose of hope, consult the royal Mouse.

*Princesses rise and shine—
never rise and whine*

Self-pity is no party. Perhaps you've thrown a "pity party" for yourself at least once in your life. Maybe you know some folks who throw one every day.

It can be easy to justify our sorrow. We feel people have done us wrong, our life is spinning out of our control, our dreams have been shattered, or we see ourselves as the victim of circumstances. So we may believe we have good reason to be down and depressed.

We need to leave this pity party because these thought patterns are toxic and never worthwhile. They will destroy your hope for a better tomorrow and stifle you into a martyr complex that will blind you from your purpose and potential. Besides, no one has a good and happy time at a pity party!

I've held a few pity parties in my life. My favorite occasion for one was when I felt unappreciated and misunderstood by my husband (although I've not had reason for this type of party in many years).

During one of my pity parties, however, I recall coming across a definition that explained self-pity doesn't come from a sense of worthiness but from a sense of unrecognized worthiness. It referred to self-pity as the response of unapplauded pride and a wounded ego.

I hated to think of myself as having a wounded ego. Was my basis for feeling unappreciated and misunderstood my hurt pride?

I may not be able to change the behavior and thoughts of the people around me, but I can change how I respond to them. Just the acknowledgement of this fact made me feel empowered and encouraged—no longer the helpless victim.

I remember the story in the Bible about the man healed at the pool of Bethesda (John 5:2–9). Now truly, if ever someone could have been justified in his feelings of self-pity, this guy would have been one. He had been an invalid for thirty-eight years. For years, he had waited by this pool to be healed. The rumor was if you were the first to get in the water when it was "troubled," you would be cured of whatever ailment you suffered.

When Jesus came upon this man, he asked him, "Would you like to get well?"

Instead of a resounding "Yes!" the man gave an excuse of why he couldn't. He said, "I can't, sir, for I have no one to put me into the pool when the water bubbles up. Someone else always gets there ahead of me."

Jesus knew this man didn't have to get into the pool to be healed. He knew God created him upright and healthy, and these qualities were his innate spiritual nature now and always. So Jesus told him, "Stand up, pick up your mat, and walk!" So, the man did. No more excuses, no more being a victim of circumstances, no more pity party.

When we feel the weight of the world is on our shoulders or we feel put upon or victimized, we can do something about our plight. I once saw a bumper sticker that read, "Do you rise and shine or rise and whine?" Whining, even when we feel it's justified, will not help—will not result in healing, progress, or resolution. Quite simply, it's a waste of your time.

We can learn to stop self-pity when it attempts to creep into our thoughts. It may be normal to at first feel sad or sorry for ourselves when things go wrong. But we can immediately turn our sorrow into positive action. We can surround ourselves with things that bring joy and happiness and experience whatever makes us laugh. We can choose thankfulness as our ticket out of self-misery. If need be, we can make a list of all the good that has ever happened in our lives. We can't feel sorrowful and grateful at the same time.

Jesus did give us instruction on how to treat those who mistreat us when he said, "Love your enemies. Let them bring out the best in you, not the worst. When someone gives you a hard time, respond with the energies of prayer for that person" (Matthew 5:44).

A wounded ego and unapplauded pride is not the best in any princess. We can leave behind anything and everything that is holding us back or keeping us down. We can rise and shine to a new day of joy, peace of mind, and infinite possibilities.

A princess's worst enemy or best ally—herself

Some say we generally meet our own expectations. In fact, whether our expectations are high or low, it could be said we will rise or fall to the occasion. This is how we live self-fulfilling prophecies.

We can be either our own worst enemy or our own best ally. Whose side are you on, ladies?

When confronted by a challenge, do you meet it head on or run away? Do you try extra hard, or do you give up easily or not even try at all? Do you resolve to do what is needed, or do you make excuses and do nothing?

If low morale has taken hold of your outlook and attitude, then you have boarded a sinking ship known as self-defeat. Any ship will sink if enough water leaks into it. Nothing will take you down faster than the negativity and pessimism that self-defeat incites.

A self-defeated princess can only see the worst side. She will say what she is not rather than what she could be. She has little or no hope that change is possible. She gripes, complains, compares, and criticizes. She thinks trying something new is pointless since she will fail or be disappointed. Either she condemns herself to be nothing, or she settles for anything but what she wants.

Consequently, the self-defeated want-to-be queen gets no joy out of life and is even more depressed about her future. She has nothing good to say about herself or her ability to achieve success. "Yes, but..." is her usual response when someone suggests she consider alternative solutions to her problems.

The bottom line is that our despair will hinder us from becoming all that we can be. The good news is we're not without help and we're never without hope. It is only bewilderment that has caused us to be mistaken in our conclusions. But a fresh and inspired viewpoint can correct our faulty and flawed notions and propel us forward.

Maybe you're tired of shooting too low for yourself—and having others who expect little for you. But what about the one who has always been in your corner? Why not raise your bar as high as your mother has it raised?

Your mother knows you have unlimited potential. Her expectation has no boundaries. Her desire for her daughter is only good. She envisions infinite possibilities. Why should your bar be lower than hers?

What if there are circumstances that would bring you down, that would stop you from reaching for your dreams, that would have you feel lonely, abandoned, isolated, worthless, incompetent, useless, cheated, defenseless or ignored? Jesus said, "The kingdom of God is within you" (Luke 17:21). Did you know this means the kingdom of God—her power, strength, knowledge—is within your reach, right now, in this very moment and circumstance? Truly, we are equipped with everything we need to conquer any foe and accomplish our goals.

We are not struggling, weak, and weary women, but rather spiritual warriors who are confident, strong, and determined. Our life has reason and purpose. We need only recognize and embrace our God-given determination, resolve, ambition, diligence, tenacity, and zeal to not only raise our bar, but reach our potential.

I've often thought how good I've been at reciting all the reasons I can't do something or why I haven't—instead of just doing whatever I needed to do to fix the problem, to accomplish my goal, to improve the situation. There is always an answer even if it is different from what we first thought was the right one. Sometimes we can do more than we realize if we give ourselves the opportunity to try. For me, this has taken many forms in my life including learning how to drive a tractor, paint a house, and drive a stick shift in an old farm truck.

Don't let negativity—pessimism, cynicism, skepticism—sink your ship. You can raise your bar and set your sights on all the good God intends for you. You can be your own best ally. You can aspire to practice your spiritual prowess, which enables you to pursue the boundless opportunities of your immense promise.

A royal decree: follow your dreams

How many times in your life have you said or thought, "I can't...."?

I have an author friend—Susan Cobb—who wrote a book titled, *Virgin Territory: How I Found My Inner Guadalupe*. The top line on the back of her book jacket reads, "Real virgins say, 'Yes!'" Her book tells not only about her saying "yes" to a move to Mexico's west coast but also about her saying "yes" to a new view of herself and her purpose. In the process, she discovered the need to do away with some old labels.

What resonated with me was the idea of giving yourself permission to think beyond the confines of what you've always done or what others have generally expected from you. This also includes permission to view yourself differently from what you've accepted for yourself.

One year I decided to say "yes" to many things that I've never said "yes" to before. This included taking a trip to Italy without my husband, adding blond highlights to my hair, wearing purple nail tips, downsizing to a smaller purse and joining a ladies Bunco group—to name only a few.

After years of saying "I can't," "I don't have time," and even "I shouldn't," I suddenly had this deep desire to say "yes" to as many new things as possible—particularly things I've never done before. At the risk of sounding selfish, I wanted to say "yes" to things that were only for me.

There have been various times in my life when I struggled with feeling trapped, overwhelmed, or stressed, as well as consumed with taking care of others. One such period was when I was a young mommy. Don't get me wrong, I sincerely loved motherhood. But I recall days when I longed to have a break—or in other words, to have a little time for myself. I was grateful to have a husband and a family nearby that allowed me to say "yes" to taking a nap, a walk, or a soaking bath; to reading a book; to joining a health club or dance class; to getting my nails or hair done; or to secluding myself in the bedroom to watch a movie.

There are times when a mother—or any woman frankly—must simply say "yes" to herself and what she needs or wants to do. Let me tell you, ladies, this is okay! We don't need to feel guilty or ashamed of wanting to do something for or by ourselves.

It's been well over a decade since I became an empty nester. When my daughter first left for college, I remember feeling that I had reached an end, and I wasn't sure what I was supposed to do with myself next. I feel like I'm still transitioning to the next chapter in my life. Furthermore, it could be that this whole idea of finding purpose, understanding our identity, and clarifying our values and ideals never reaches some grand finale. Perhaps, there is no end to the discovery of who we are, because it's a lifelong journey.

I can live with that! In fact, this truth gives me permission to make changes regardless of my age.

So, any labels that I've grown accustomed to as descriptions of "me" don't have to remain sewn into my collar. Sometimes labels are imposed upon us that don't genuinely represent our style, tastes, preferences, interests, or values. Maybe we simply want to consider new ideas and inspirations. Why do we ever believe we can't make a change?

I think giving yourself permission is about being honest with yourself throughout your life. It's about not boxing yourself into a set-in-stone self-image, a set of viewpoints and opinions, or even settling for a job that you no longer want. It's also about realizing that possibilities and opportunities don't diminish with age.

The more I eradicate limiting labels, the more I see the world in color instead of black and white. What a lovely world I am finding—a world that is flexible, adaptable, resilient, creative, inspired, imaginative, receptive, open, unobstructed, unrestricted, boundless.

Dear princesses and queens, give yourself permission to do or be whatever you're dreaming of or longing for. You may find saying "Yes!" and "I can!" feels pretty darn good.

Rulers look ahead, not behind

I should have... I could have... If only I would have...

How much time do you spend thinking about what might have been? This is a question that reminds me of a favorite country/western song. The lyrics include the phrases, "I try not to think about what might have been, cause that was then / There's no way to know what might have been." Even though we all probably know better, we still have times when we lament and pine over what might have been.

I've read that the biggest secret regret is omission—not doing something you feel you should have done. It seems we are often haunted by the inactions of our lives. But harboring regret is not good for your health and can lead to depression and even physical illness.

Are there ever times when regret is positive and helpful? The lessons that can come with regrets and the wisdom we glean can help us make changes so we don't repeat mistakes or bad choices.

Call it failed expectations or perhaps lost opportunities, I've struggled at times to overcome feelings of regret. When I shared these feelings with my husband John one day, he asked me, "What would you have done differently?" The crazy thing is that I didn't have an answer. It's not that I wanted to change any particular one thing in my life. I've loved every moment of my life to this day. At the time, for no apparent reason, I was overcome with sadness and disappointment that somehow I've missed doing something or that it was too late to do some things.

I finally concluded that rehashing regret served no good purpose. I could see that regret interferes with happy, productive living and restricts motivation to move forward. I realized if there was something I really wanted to do, that I could do it. Nothing was stopping me but my own inaction.

For a while after my daughter first returned home during her divorce proceedings, she felt in limbo with no idea what she should do with her life. But I believe that God is always working out her purpose in our life. There is no reason to ever think that her plan is not going to continue for the remainder of our days. I don't believe there is an end to God's direction or the goodness she provides, so, as I explained to my daughter, we don't need to fear any such end just because we've reached some pinnacle moment or crossroad in our life.

It can be difficult at such times to even begin to imagine all the good that God has in store for us. As Paul says, "Eye hath not seen, not ear heard, neither have entered into the heart of man, the things which God hath prepared for them that love [her]" (1 Corinthians 2:9).

It helps to begin with our view of God. This view can help free us from any stifling feelings of needless regret. God is infinite good, and we are the expression of the infinite. Everything God gives is also infinite. Sometimes we may think of our experiences, or possibilities for experiences, as somehow finite. Yet God provides infinite possibilities for blessing our lives.

We can change our view of self from being limited or bewildered to what God is surely always knowing for us. This viewpoint will enable us to see the unfathomable prospects that are present now and in the future—opportunities that bring joy, fun, fulfillment, satisfaction, and a sense of accomplishment. So, put "what might have been" behind you and focus your gaze on what is yet to be—on what you shall do, what you can do, what you will do. It's going to be wonderful.

Never doubt your greatness

You are worthy, and your life is worthwhile. Never doubt this!

No person or thing can undermine the talents and skills that are uniquely yours—not a teacher, friend, parent, spouse, or employer, not even your age or circumstance.

I have sometimes allowed myself to be saddened and depressed by something someone has said to me. I've let another's words make me feel inconsequential, useless, and of no purpose. But the truth is no one has the right or ability to stifle your dreams, bruise your spirit, question your interests, or dictate your choices. It is impossible, unless you give someone the power to do so.

Your thoughts, opinions, and viewpoints are yours, and they are special. They have the right to exist and be acted upon. God created you with the ability to think, and no one can think for you.

Over the years I've changed my priorities, my goals, and my wishes to fit the needs and wants of others. When I met my husband, I was planning to get my law degree. But after we married, it was decided we would live on his family's cattle ranch.

I decided to change my career goals and become a teacher. I'm not saying this was a wrong decision, but I do sometimes wonder what I would have done if I had not married when I did.

When I reached what many refer to as "mid-life," I was feeling dissatisfied. I was questioning the merit of what I had accomplished in my life, and I longed for something more. Yet I was uncertain of what it would take to satisfy that longing.

I discovered that when we allow our worthiness to come into question, we dampen our motivation and lower our expectation that it is possible to reach dreams and accomplish goals. Thus, our feelings of unworthiness can become a self-fulfilling prophecy.

What would have happened if Moses had let his doubts about his worthiness to free the children of Israel stop him from trying? Remember how Moses responded when God told him he was being sent to Pharaoh? Moses asked, "Who am I that I should go to Pharaoh? (Exodus 3:11).

Undoubtedly, the task seemed like a huge undertaking. I suppose Moses was uncertain he had what it would take to get the job done. I love knowing that God promised Moses she would always be with him. Although this news was reassuring, Moses continued to express his doubts as he and God further discussed the plans for his mission. Moses protested, "The people won't believe me. I am not eloquent. I am slow of speech." But God had an answer for each concern Moses interjected.

Sometimes I think we can become our own worst enemy as we distrust our abilities and debunk our potential. Yet I concluded from reading about Moses that not only does God have a mission for each of us, she can provide us with everything we need to accomplish the mission. At least that help was there for

Moses! I like to believe that surely she can help the rest of us reach our goals, too.

I say, "Never doubt your worth or worthiness. Never doubt your abilities." I have always believed that God not only will give us what we need, she's going to lead us, she has our back, and she'll hold our hand. The queen of good advice in my life, my mamma, has always assured me that God is with us every step of our life journey. No matter what need arises along the way, God would have a solution. My mamma has always been right!

Our journeys are our own. Each princess and queen has a purpose that is significant. Each of our missions is distinct. No one else is suitable or worthy to fulfill our individual mission. Don't let anyone make you believe otherwise.

A queen asks, "Why not?"

Change—some people dread it, and others can't get enough. It may be much like the adage, "One man's trash is another man's treasure." When it comes to what we would alter or why we would make a modification, the answers vary because we all have different things we value, want, need, and consider important.

I'm one of those queens who can't get enough change. Even when I'm not actively seeking it, I feel a hunger for it. This often results in my imagination working overtime, wondering what I could change—replace, remodel, reorganize, improve, or do differently.

There are things I would never trade about my life. I adore my husband—one fact that is firm and fixed. Unfortunately, my dear husband is one of those folks who dreads change, so there are times his feelings impact what I can change about our life together.

Furthermore, sometimes what I think I might like to change and what I feel I can or would are different. When this happens to any of us, I think it's important to examine why we feel we can't or wouldn't make a change.

In other words, what's stopping you?

When I mention to my husband something I'm thinking about changing, he often responds with, "Why now?" My response to him is always, "Why not?"

I've told my daughter that I think it's the "Why not?" question that must be answered when we're hesitant to make a change. If I find my hesitancy is based on a fear, that's when I become determined to conquer the fear. Answering this question and conquering my fears is what helped me take that trip to Italy with my girlfriend—without husbands going with us.

Many times in my life I've let fear stop me from reaching some goal or aspiration. Since I can't go back and change all the things I wish I had done and living in regret is completely pointless, today my resolve is fierce when I'm faced with a fear that is trying to hold me back.

Now, I do believe in making informed decisions. There could be information that might stop me from making a change.

It could also be that some changes are better at one time than at another. If a desired change shouldn't happen today, it doesn't mean that at some point in the future it couldn't or shouldn't happen.

But one thing is for sure—do not let fear paralyze you with uncertainty, indecisiveness, and inaction. You must stop fear before it stops you.

It's helpful to look at your fear straight on and examine what it is telling you. Perhaps your fear is saying: "You can't do it or it will be too difficult." "You're afraid of what others will think." "You will fail." "You will be wrong." "You won't like the outcome."

Some people say that fear can be rational and logical and is a helpful instinct that protects us from danger. I don't think it is fear that makes decisions and actions rational, logical, and safe, but rather knowledge, understanding, and common sense, as well as divine inspiration and revelation.

At least from my own experience, fear is irrational and baseless. It is some illusive belief that would stop me from making my life better—happier, more satisfying, more interesting, more productive, more fun.

Changes are natural—and can be progressive—throughout our lives. Making a well-thought-out change need not be feared but welcomed, explored, and enjoyed.

I always say asking yourself "Why not?" when considering some change can be very telling. You may find that there isn't a good enough reason not to.

Even in a castle, some days are like that

So you had a bad day. Do you want to relive it by replaying the details of each bad scene over and over again in your head? Both my mamma and I have struggled with this, and I hope my daughter doesn't follow in our footsteps.

I realize that some bad days seem tough to leave behind us. Maybe we're consumed with regrets, filled with frustrations, battered with self-condemnation, or overwhelmed with depression.

What can we do to cut through the mire of agony that is bringing us down? Is there an antidote for bad days?

I guess there are many types of bad days. Perhaps the most common is when all that makes up our own unique minutiae goes wrong. You know, the day-to-day details—the particulars that form much of your day.

When I was a teacher aide during college, I was introduced to a book that I was to read to a class of second graders. Little did I know that it would become a book that would change how I looked at my life for the rest of my life.

There is an antidote for bad days, and its secret is tucked away in that children's book. When I made the discovery, I wasn't surprised that a children's book could hold such valuable and insightful knowledge. Just look at children. They seem to be experts at falling down and jumping right back up again, perhaps after brushing the dirt off their pants first. Then they immediately go right back to doing what they were doing before their fall. Isn't this called resilience?

What's the name of this miracle book, you ask? None other than *Alexander and the Terrible, Horrible, No Good, Very Bad Day*, written by Judith Viorst.

As the story develops, Alexander has one of those bad days we can all probably relate to. Shortly after his morning began, he concluded, "I could tell it was going to be a terrible, horrible, no good, very bad day." You might reach this same conclusion too if you woke up with gum in your hair, tripped on a skateboard as you got out of bed, and dropped the sweater you were planning to wear that day in the sink while the water was running. Before he even had breakfast, he could predict what his day was going to be like.

His day does seem to go from bad to worse. Nothing was to go poor Alexander's way. From getting smashed in the middle seat of the car, a dessertless lunch sack, a cavity at the dentist office, forced to own stripeless sneakers, lima beans for dinner, witnessing kissing on television, being made to sleep in railroad-train pajamas, and so much more. Alexander's day went so bad, several times he considers moving to Australia.

However, by the day's end, Alexander reaches a simple conclusion that reveals the secret to overcoming bad days. He said, "My mom says some days are like that. Even in Australia." You get the feeling he turns over and goes peacefully to sleep, leaving his bad day far behind him.

The key to overcoming bad days is having a childlike, resilient attitude. Guess what? All queens and princesses have it.

Yes, we royal women are buoyant, adaptable, adjustable, flexible. This makes us able to recover strength, spirits, and good humor quickly. When something tries to get us down, we are able to bounce promptly back up.

Queens are perfectly capable of remaining spiritually lighthearted. This gives us dominion over all the "earthiness" of life—which includes all the minutiae of our castle days.

Maintaining a spiritually lighthearted, resilient attitude is possible and powerful. I've been testing its potency since my discovery of Alexander's book over twenty-five years ago. When embraced, this state of mind can calmly cut through any bad day we have to face.

Happiness comes with the territory

I heard someone say that Amazon.com boasts more than 20,000 titles on the subject of happiness. Yet with all the reading we're doing, many of us will still say we haven't found it yet.

Some say a deep longing for happiness is at the heart of the desire for money, fame, and power. Perhaps the best advice anyone could give us, whether we're married or single, is to stop waiting for happiness to come galloping over the next horizon.

From my own experience, happiness does not come from trying to be someone different than who we are, nor in running from here to somewhere else. Happiness is not in the things we desire nor is it based on conditions. Happiness is always within our reach, but to have it we must sometimes take a stand and mentally fight for our divine right to be happy.

This is not a new discovery or one only discovered by me. Several other folks have reached a similar conclusion. Abraham Lincoln said, "People are about as happy as they make up their minds to be." Roman Emperor Marcus Antonius said, "No man is happy who does not think himself so." English journalist

Roger L'Estrange said, "It is not the place nor the condition, but the mind alone that can make anyone happy or miserable."

My daughter has sometimes been skeptical at the idea that you can be happy regardless of your conditions and circumstances—especially while going through her divorce. There were many days when she sighed, "What is there to be happy about?" She would then proceed to share her long list of reasons why she couldn't possibly be happy.

But I have proven to myself that a change in attitude and viewpoint leads to a change in perspective and outlook, which inevitably results in improved situations. Living next door to in-laws who, in my early marriage years, often made me feel they weren't pleased with my husband's choice in a wife gave me many opportunities for implementing my attitude adjustment.

I love the old story of the gatekeeper, which for me beautifully drives home the idea that your thoughts will make you happy or unhappy no matter where you are. I shared this story with my daughter during one of her melancholy days.

There was a gatekeeper to a small town. One day a visitor came to the gate and asked, "What kind of town is this?"

The gatekeeper asked the visitor, "From what kind of town did you come?"

The inquirer reported his town was one of dissatisfaction, disharmony, and disgust, to which the gatekeeper responded, "You will find this town to be the same."

Sadly, the visitor went on his way somewhere else.

The next day another visitor arrived at the gate and asked the gatekeeper about his town.

Again the gatekeeper asked, "From what kind of town did you come?"

This visitor gave a glowing report of his former home telling of the love, the sharing, and the goodwill of its inhabitants.

To this report the gatekeeper exclaimed, "Come in! This place will be just as that from which you came."

Happiness is not found in running from here to somewhere else. Whether here or somewhere else, happiness must be found within or we'll never permanently be happy. You take with you what you've packed!

I believe happiness must be as consciously practiced as gratitude, forgiveness, and kindness. As with everything else, the more we practice it, the better we get at it. When need be, we must defend and argue for our divine right to be happy and not allow anything to rob us or stop us from being happy.

As I've said before, the Psalmist proclaims, "This is the day which the Lord hath made, we will rejoice and be glad in it" (Psalms 118:24). But it's a couple of verses prior that give us some reasons why our divine right to happiness is assured: "The Lord is on our side" (Psalms 118:6) and "The Lord is our strength and song" (Psalms 118:14).

Two of the biggest deterrents to our happiness, ladies, begin with "I could, if..." or "I can't." Try beginning your day with "I will" and see what happens. I believe that God wants us all to be happy. That means being happy ourselves and bringing happiness to others in spite of anything trying to steal our joy.

Part Four
Going for goals

113 | Introduction
115 | Conquer that dastardly dragon—the schedule
118 | Ants—ruled by queens; royal examples
121 | Multitasking mindfully in the throne room
124 | A queen is not afraid of her own voice
127 | Treasure the beauty all around you
130 | Outlaw energy leaks in all the land
133 | Sometimes commanding means abandoning the plan
136 | Keep a little fun on your court agenda

Going for goals — Introduction

Setting goals and striving to reach them is something every princess will experience. The truth is, goals are not limited to a certain time in one's life. My daughter Jennifer had one set of goals when she first left home for college, a brand new set of goals after she married, and then different ones again after her divorce. I can say the same for my own life. My goals have changed multiple times, often influenced by life's occasions—after college, after getting married, after having a baby, when we began homeschooling, after my daughter left for college, when I resigned from my job, when my daughter returned home after her divorce, and so on.

One reason going for goals is a lifetime proposition is we're never too young or old to achieve something new. Jennifer once shared with me one of her favorite quotes, which gives a list of accomplishments by various people at various ages: "At age 7, Mozart wrote his first symphony. At 12, Shane Gould won an Olympic medal. At 14, Leann Rimes topped the country music charts. At 17, Joan of Arc led an army in defense of Europe. At 57, Ray Kroc founded McDonalds. At 71, Michelangelo painted the Sistine Chapel. At 80, George Burns won his first Oscar. At 104,

Cal Evans wrote his first book on the American West" (*I Believe in You,* compiled by Dan Zadra).

Having passed the mid-century mark myself, I find a lot of encouragement in this list. I love the idea that it's never too late to make new goals and then reach them.

Jennifer gained a provocative perspective during her first ten years away from home. She says she now believes that living the life of our dreams never reaches a final destination. So, our lifetime is always ahead of us. This is undoubtedly why, when I wondered aloud one day about all the things I wanted to do in my life and hadn't, she asked me, "What would you like to do?" Then she insisted, "Do it!"

I've loved watching my daughter set her goals and check them off her list one by one after she accomplished them. She has acquired a can-do attitude that is convinced anything is doable and attainable. She inspires me to believe the same—even now.

I've not yet become the person I've always wanted to be. But on that note, maybe we're always in the state of "becoming." We never reach the point where we can say there's nothing more to learn or experience or achieve.

I probably don't need to remind my daughter to never stop dreaming and striving to accomplish her dreams. I know she won't! But this same reminder is good for us mothers, too.

The essays that follow explore many topics I hope will be helpful as you strive to reach your goals: setting priorities, having the perseverance needed, multi-tasking, overcoming shyness, time management, dealing with stress, planning skills, and remembering to have fun while you go for your crown.

Conquer that dastardly dragon — the schedule

My husband John inadvertently taught me a lesson years ago on how to set priorities and keep them.

It's rare that two social events capture John's interest in the same weekend. The first was the premiere of a movie he wanted to see—a James Bond movie—and the second, a concert by one of his favorite musicians—Ray Wylie Hubbard.

The problem with this scenario was that this weekend would also be a busy hay-baling weekend. For anyone not familiar with what this means, he would have days so full of cutting, raking, baling, and hauling hundreds of hay bales that he would have little time to add more activities to his schedule.

During hay season he has generally told me he could make no promises on our social agenda. This particular weekend was different because our social agenda concerned him more than it did me.

Now don't get me wrong. I was interested in doing these activities almost as much as my husband. But I would not have been as disappointed if we didn't do them. It became clear as Friday came around, that come hell, hay, or high water, we were going to the movies that day. Indeed we did, as well as the concert on Saturday evening. John finished baling on Saturday thirty minutes before we needed to leave. My man cleans up fast when highly motivated.

My husband's actions showed that the best way to determine how to set priorities could be to ask some questions. What matters most to us or what will we make time for—no matter what, in any event, in any case? What are we determined to do even if it is difficult? In other words, come hell, hay, or high water, what ranks at the top of our preferences, what takes precedence, what has our highest regard, what is our greatest concern, what will sway us into immediate action, what is so paramount that we can't live without it? I suspect you get the idea.

This type of questioning can help us set priorities that are truly significant and important to us. With priorities that have our utmost concern, we will be motivated to action. We will set goals that we are impelled to accomplish, yes, come hell, hay, or high water. I suspect our time management skills would also greatly improve.

It's interesting that it seems the source of the phrase "hell or high water" may have had its beginnings in the early 1900s during the cattle drives, when cowboys herded their longhorns through high water of rivers and endured the hell of trail conditions between rivers. The original phrase was "in spite of hell and high water."

Perhaps in spite of hell and high water speaks more about the determination required to accomplish a mission, reach a goal, and maintain priorities. This brings to mind a long list of qualities such as persistence, perseverance, firmness, tenacity, resolve, fortitude, courage, boldness, stamina, steadiness, and drive.

I think that a person striving to accomplish her goals and dreams or reach her destination, in spite of hell and high water, has clarity of intention, purpose, reason, motive and rationale. Consequently, this person will be able to stay focused on her direction and objective, and she will let nothing stop her from doing what she must—again, come hell, hay, or high water.

As I said, I learned a lesson that weekend about setting priorities—and also what it means to maintain them. Our priorities are important, ladies. They need to be preserved and at times defended—I'll say it one more time—come hell, hay, or high water.

Ants—ruled by queens; royal examples

Living up on a ranch, I can tell you that ants—fire ants in particular—are no friend to farmers and ranchers. My husband John concurs. Each year he faces what feels like a losing battle trying to smooth our pastures due to the ever-increasing number of ant mounds. Somehow it feels like an oxymoron to suggest that ants, one of the smallest and most annoying of God's creatures, know the key to being successful. Perhaps this, too, is why they seem impossible to get rid of!

Consider this lesson about the ant that you can read in the Bible: "You lazy fool, look at an ant. Watch it closely; let it teach you a thing or two. Nobody has to tell it what to do. All summer it stores up food; at harvest it stockpiles provisions. So how long are you going to laze around doing nothing?" (Proverbs 6:6–9).

Do you ever desire to be more productive in your work? Do you ever feel overwhelmed, frustrated, bored, or afraid to take some necessary steps in your life or career?

There have been times when I've struggled with a lack of motivation to complete a project. Sometimes I've lacked the motivation to begin. There have been other times when I have felt so overwhelmed and stretched by the demands upon me that I reached my limit of endurance. Believe it or not, pondering the life and works of the ant gave me fresh inspiration and helped me overcome difficult times in my life.

My view of ants is that they know their purpose in life very well and seem to keep it in the forefront of their thought as they keep moving. Now bear with me on this analogy. I doubt that ants actually have emotions or thoughts. I'm just imagining details from watching these annoying pests in action. It appears to me that they don't allow anything to interfere with their purpose. Obstacles in their path do not stop them. They refuse to give up. For me, they are examples of courage, expectancy, and determination.

Once a task is complete, ants go immediately to the next job at hand. Ants appear to approach each undertaking with zest, energy, enthusiasm. Persistence may be their greatest characteristic. I suspect ants would never consider defeat. They face unexpected tasks with confidence and resolve. I have no doubt they will not stop until their goal is reached.

Ants don't work or live alone. They embody the concept of teamwork. They're innately programmed to behave as though their own success requires others around them to be successful, too. Therefore, any ant is ever ready to help a fellow ant. They are always ready to lend aid and support.

They can carry objects that weigh enough to crush them, and yet they appear to carry these heavy loads effortlessly. Perhaps the old adage about the joy in your steps making everything lighter is something the ant puts into practice.

Mary Baker Eddy was not speaking about ants, but her words in an essay titled, "Fidelity" seem quite fitting to me: "The conscientious are successful. They follow faithfully; through evil or through good report, they work on to the achievement of good;

by patience, they inherit the promise. Be active, and however slow, thy success is sure: toil is triumph; and—thou has been faithful over a few things."

It's emulating the many qualities that an ant exemplifies—such as diligence, patience, perseverance, and persistence—that helps me climb over those pesky hills called boredom, fear, or frustration and prove that conscientious effort results in success. I can say that it took all the diligence and perseverance I could muster to complete projects and meet deadlines when I worked in public relations, and it always takes everything I've got to get our income tax submitted on time. Frankly, it requires a lot of persistence to keep up with our dirty laundry!

Dear daughters, I hope you too will find inspiration and encouragement for your endeavors from the life of an ant.

Multitasking mindfully in the throne room

I've often heard on television news that Americans are multi-taskers and we're proud of it. Many people seem to believe that they are sufficiently skilled to handle multiple tasks simultaneously, alternating from job to job in rapid speed. Although on the surface they appear more efficient, in their haste they may actually be taking more time to reach their goals and sacrificing quality as well.

No matter how much folks try to convince themselves or even how much evidence there may be to the contrary, I personally do not believe a person can do multiple things at the same time and do them well. Or at least, I'm not good at it! I agree with what Clint Eastwood says at the end of one of his Dirty Harry movies: "A man's gotta know his limitations."

I have friends whose companies have let employees go while expecting those remaining to pick up the slack. Some businesses have the mantra, "Do more with less." I think multitasking—trying to accomplish several duties at once—may in fact reduce productivity, not increase it.

I recall a segment on Oprah a few years ago that discussed the steep price tag that comes with multitasking. A wife shared how she felt she never had her husband's full attention because he brought his work home with him—constantly checking his BlackBerry, answering his cell phone, and checking messages and emails. Imagine how your coworker, friend, spouse, lover, or child would feel if every time they said something to you, you turned and gave them all of your attention—without thinking about what was next on your to-do list?

It seems to me that we really don't multitask—we juggle. Yet we can only do one task at a time. Whether we complete our various responsibilities quickly or slowly, we're still only working on one endeavor at a time. The problem is that no one undertaking has our attention for very long because we must focus immediately on the next item on our list. The more we juggle, the greater the odds that we will drop some "ball." Yet, juggling fewer duties or decreasing our priorities is not always the only answer.

Longing for a solution to multitasking madness myself, I turned to Jesus' life and his three-year career. Here was a man who accomplished much in his brief ministry and whose eternal legacy still transforms the world generations after his work was completed. He taught and healed multitudes during those three years. How did he do so much in such a short period?

I decided to examine his typical workdays for insight. The book of Luke, chapter 8 tells about many activities over what appears to be a very short amount of time—perhaps a day or a few days. During this time, Jesus traveled back and forth between two regions by boat, spoke to a large crowd, taught disciples in a private session, calmed a storm at sea, healed a madman, raised a little girl from death, and healed a woman with an issue of blood on the way to heal the little girl. All of this in only one chapter!

While it appeared that Jesus juggled many tasks, he really was about a single mission and purpose. His only work was being about his Father's business. He never lost sight of this, regardless of the numerous details presenting themselves to him. This enabled him to focus on the needs of the moment and be responsive to each person he met. Jesus was flexible, adjustable, listening, discerning. I can't imagine Jesus as rushed, pressured, stressed out, or overwhelmed. I think he calmly went about accomplishing his work, fully attentive to each and every moment.

No, I don't believe Jesus practiced multitasking to accomplish his great mission—but, rather, the art of mindful living.

Perhaps the key to our success is to adopt "the mind of Christ" as Paul says (Philippians 2:5). This means we, too, should give our full attention to every moment and each person during those moments. We make mindfulness our approach to each day and every endeavor. I suspect such a mindful approach in our work and everyday life would result in greater achievement, fulfillment, satisfaction, and happiness.

A queen is not afraid of her own voice

My daughter often told me that in her freshmen college classes there were times when she wanted to participate in a discussion and shyness kept her from doing so. I know she has diligently worked to overcome any shy tendencies that would keep her from being successful in college. She has been successful in her endeavors.

There have been many times in my life when I allowed shyness to hold me back. There were the boys in school that I longed to be friends with, but I would never dare make eye contact with them. There was the part in the school play I would have loved to have auditioned for, but I didn't. There were the questions the teacher asked I could have answered, but I never raised my hand.

It doesn't matter how you define it, I believe shyness is rooted in fear. Fear of rejection, humiliation, loss, or failure incites shyness—or perhaps I could say—insecurity.

It's no different than when we allow ourselves to become introverted, sheepish, timid, and guarded after a relationship ends badly or unexpectedly. If it was a bad experience, we may be questioning our judgment and doubting our ability to make a better choice in the future. If death ended a relationship, we may be afraid we will face loss and grief again. Either way, the result is probably the same—shyness that results in being cowardly, wary, and alone.

The problem with being shy is that the impact is far-reaching. We are not the only one who loses or is hurt.

I recall reading about a basketball coach who explained how hesitation and timidity leads to passing the ball. He said, "If a player has an open shot that she can make, and she decides to pass instead, that player is being selfish and hurting the team." Fear of failure would obstruct this basketball player from her likely success, the coach further explained, and could cost her team the game win.

Other people need you. They need your intelligence, insight, skills, talents, and help. Hiding behind shyness, you limit the benefit you can be to others.

Shyness almost always causes us to believe negative assumptions, and these assumptions are almost always wrong. This is especially true when we believe that the other person will not like us or will not be interested in what we have to say. Our fear will intimidate us into missing an opportunity to make a new friend. The fact is other people may have the same fears and inhibitions we do.

I've often been inspired by the story of Ruth in the Bible. Ruth was described as a warmhearted and unselfish woman who trusted and loved her mother-in-law very much. After Ruth's husband passed away suddenly, Ruth traveled with her mother-in-law back to her homeland.

This was a more gracious act by Ruth than it might sound. Her mother-in-law Naomi was not only a widow, but all of her sons had died as well. She would have been traveling alone to her homeland if Ruth had not returned with her. Plus, Ruth had to be courageous to go to an unfamiliar land and be around people she had never met before—especially during a time when she was facing her own grief and uncertainty as a young widow.

I love the fact that Ruth was willing to embrace a new experience. She didn't over-think or speculate about her future. She didn't wallow in her doubts. Even though she had no idea what would happen next, she moved forward.

Ruth and Naomi arrived at their destination. Among strangers in a strange land, Ruth could have been apprehensive, anxious, nervous, and cautious, but she wasn't. She boldly took initiative to gather food in nearby fields. She even, without hesitation, asked one of the women gleaning grain near her for the name of the man who spoke kindly as he went by. It turned out the man Boaz was the owner of the field.

I bet you can guess the happy ending to this story. Ruth and Boaz soon married, and Ruth's mother-in-law lived with them and helped care for the son they eventually had. Their son, by the way, would become the grandfather to the famous King David.

Sometimes a shy person will say self-consciousness keeps them quiet. But I would say, what self are you being conscious of?

Listen up, princesses! You are the woman of God's creating—made in her image. Your innate nature includes the qualities of poise, confidence, strength, courage, compassion, love. Be true to yourself. Happiness is found in being who God made you to be.

You can do it. Your thinking is your most powerful weapon. Use it. Follow your heart. Don't hide your light and love. Be the spiritual self that God intended. Don't be shy. Be yourself—freely, unconditionally, and fearlessly. You'll be much happier if you do.

Treasure the beauty all around you

I often suffer from self-imposed tunnel vision. This means my visual field and focus becomes severely constricted. In fact, I've had friends walking toward me who practically had to tackle me to get my attention.

Once upon a time a forwarded email gave me reason to re-evaluate the pace of my life. I forwarded this email to my daughter, who had become super busy balancing her college graduate classes, work, and a social life.

The email told about when the *Washington Post* conducted a social experiment that won them a Pulitzer for a story published in April 2007. The feature told about a cold January morning when a man sat at a metro station in Washington, D.C., and played the violin. He played six Bach pieces for forty-five minutes. Of the thousands of people who saw and heard this man, only six stopped and stayed for a while, and about twenty gave him money as they continued to walk their normal pace. The one who paid the most attention was a three-year-old child, but his mom soon forced him to move along. He did this reluctantly, turning his head back as he walked in order to see the violinist. It seems several other children also repeated this action.

It turns out the man playing incognito was violin virtuoso Joshua Bell.

The concluding question of the email was: "If we do not have a moment to stop and listen to one of the best musicians in the world playing the best music ever written, how many other things are we missing?"

When I finished reading the email, I was immediately reminded of one of my husband's favorite country songs by Alabama titled, "I'm in a Hurry (and Don't Know Why)." I usually don't know why either.

My husband suggested that perhaps many of the people were on their way to work and maybe even running late so they couldn't have stopped to listen to the violinist even if they had wanted to. I suppose this might have been the case.

But are there times when we should "stop to hear the music"?

Must our obligations and responsibilities keep us from taking time to appreciate what's happening around us? Should we ever be so busy that we're unavailable to our friends and family, unable to find the time for a sunset or a single mindful breath?

On that cold day in January 2007 in Washington, D.C., thousands were so busy or in such a hurry they missed a free opportunity to hear music that two days before people in Boston paid an average of $100 to hear.

I decided I didn't want to be that busy anymore. My new priority became to experience life more fully. I wanted to grasp each moment of my day. I wanted to take time to look around and give my full attention to those I'm with. I wanted to eat slower and take more walks. I wanted more time to simply be quiet, to reflect, to ponder, to pray.

I wanted to give more time to having fun—and fun I've been having! I enjoy each and every day. I don't feel rushed when talking with family or friends over the telephone. I feel more satisfied with my life than ever before. If I don't get something done I had planned to do one day, I'm perfectly happy with waiting till the next day or even next week, for that matter. No longer is time the director of my days!

How often do you refrain from acting on an urge to do something fun because you are so busy that you don't have time?

No more of that for me. I plan to hear more music every day, every year for the rest of my life. I hope that all of you princesses do, too!

Outlaw energy leaks in all the land

None of us want to waste the precious times of our life, but I suspect we've probably all been guilty of doing just that. I know both my daughter and I would hate to admit how much time we've wasted being mad, unhappy, depressed, frustrated, indecisive, complaining, or feeling discouraged or overwhelmed.

How do we combat these enemies to our joy, peace, progress, and success?

I've never forgotten an idea a friend shared with me a few years ago—"Jesus avoided energy leaks." (Learn more here: www.heartwiseministries.org/relationship/devotionals.)

I agreed with that assertion. "Energy leaks" to me meant those things that would deter Jesus, distract him, or stop him from doing his work. He had a clear sense of his mission and his purpose. He was steadfast and centered. I don't think Jesus was ever willful or headstrong. (I can't say the same!) Since his work involved obediently following God's direction, he had to remain ever prayerful and listening for his next instructions.

It seems to me that Jesus maintained his spiritual energy, never allowing any "leaks" that would pull his thought and attention away from his focus. This kept him in a state of readiness, flexibility, openness, and willingness.

My friend offered this idea about Jesus, trying to help me get through what seemed like a day of impossible roadblocks at work. It was a day of time constraints, confusion, unclear communication, and backtracking. Ever experience a day like that?

I was just about ready to write the day off as hopeless. At the peak of my frustration, this idea of Jesus not allowing any "energy leaks" was compelling. I had been letting the energy leaks of stress, fear, irritability, and misunderstanding hold sway. I was running on low fuel, so the thought of being able to stop energy leaks was very desirable.

I considered how Jesus remained calm and focused on his work when confronted by multitudes with many different needs. Or how he was able to express dominion and confident resolve while doing his work even in the midst of angry and jealous peers.

Deciding perhaps it was possible for me to take the example of Jesus as my problem-solving model, I began a new approach that very day with each calamity that presented itself. This required a response change on my part—to remain calm regardless of the circumstance. It worked! With the calming of any would-be anxieties, stress, or pressure that threatened to bring productivity to a halt came peace, freshness, and new views—spiritual energy. I felt refueled to tackle anything.

With additional challenges—and there were more that day—solutions came quickly. I resolved to maintain my spiritual poise and not allow any "energy leaks." What a day! Instead of a day of everything going wrong, much was accomplished and deadlines were reached.

I've often thought about the lessons learned that day.

There are many enemies to our joy and peace—sickness, pain, worries, and a myriad of fears. But my spiritual energy lesson has taught me that a calm and spiritually poised response leads to healing and progress. I suspect as we're successful at not allowing any energy leaks, we'll find we are prepared and equipped to handle whatever comes our way.

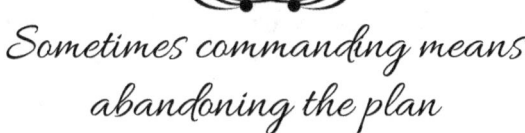

Sometimes commanding means abandoning the plan

My daughter Jennifer has learned to go with the flow of her many responsibilities and tasks—and without a to-do list. She is flexible and easily adaptable to whatever a situation may require. She does everything she needs to get done almost always in record-breaking time. She does a great job! She manages stress very well with her approach. She does not take after her mother when her mother was her age.

How have I planned my life? Oh, let me count the ways...

I had a plan for where I would go to college, whom I would marry, when I would marry, how many children I would have, when I would have my first child, when I would have the second child, and so on. I've had a plan for every day of my life. From the time I would wake up until the time I went to bed, I had a schedule and a to-do list. Each task on my to-do list had its own detailed plan of action.

But I'm not finished yet.

I've made my Christmas gift list months in advance. In fact, I've worried about everything months in advance.

Every vacation had an itinerary and, of course, an extensive list of items to take along.

I've even made plans for other people in my life, including for my husband and daughter. I don't think I've ever made a move in my life without a plan or without probably two back-up plans to boot.

Not all my plans worked out in the exact way I had planned them. But my solace has always been, "Well, at least I had a plan."

Having goals isn't bad. They have their usefulness. But I've wondered if I could have used more meandering in my days gone by. Perhaps I could have set up fewer boundaries or directives for the possibilities of my life. My vision for my life has had way too many limits, as well as blinders.

You see, my own vision had often been too narrow. I could only foresee the future given what had gone before. I couldn't account in my plan for the wonderful, surprising turns life could take. If I stuck rigidly to my own plan, I could miss out.

Part of my problem with being a planner was illustrated by how devastated I was when a plan fell short, when I was unable to handle the unknown, or when I wasn't flexible enough to enact a plan that wasn't my own.

Eventually, I began to see that God has a plan for our lives that has an infinite design. Within infinitude, there can be no limits, no boundaries, no restrictions, no inadequacies, and even no defined specifics. That's right. I no longer feel that God has one specific plan for my life. I don't believe Mother Love thinks in terms of human details. Why would she? Or could she? I think God's view of her creation could only reflect her own nature. There are no limits or lack in the infinite divine. There surely can't be any with what the divine creates.

What does this mean for me these days?

I haven't turned into a "fly by the seat of my pants" kind of queen. But, there is more appeal to that idea now. I am more open-minded about my future and what choices I make. In fact, I want to have days when I have no list whatsoever in front of me. I want to go on a trip and have no idea what I'm going to do on any given day. Actually, I would love to take a trip and have no map, no compass, no headings, and no familiar landmarks. Just head out and go where the wind blows, as they say.

Coming from me, a longtime planner, these ideas would probably sound radical to my daughter. I've come to believe that perhaps the greatest plan is one that anticipates being astonished.

A sense of wonder and awe may be the most special outcomes of maintaining an infinite point of view—one that is always ready to seize unexpected moments and opportunities. I can only imagine how happy a life of being surprised each morning at the beautiful sunrise—whether a cloudy or sunny day—would be. I'm trying to imagine being delighted with each phone call I receive—no matter how many times my phone rings each day. Or to gracefully receive each and every event in my life—not being daunted, overwhelmed, or exasperated when every detail doesn't pan out the way I envisioned.

I am happy to no longer be such a compulsive planner and to be more spontaneous and open to the untold potential in every aspect and each moment of my life.

If you're going to plan, I say be sure you plan to be surprised. That's my plan!

Keep a little fun on your court agenda

Were you among the three million people who watched the YouTube video of the piano stairs? Volkswagen had initiated the "fun theory," which asserted that fun is the easiest way to change people's behavior for the better. There was a contest that explored such questions as "Can fun make more people exercise?" (www.thefuntheory.com).

I wasn't surprised that turning stairs into a larger-than-life piano resulted in more people taking the stairs rather than the escalator. I would definitely choose the musical option as the fun way to go.

What's your idea of fun?

Longing to learn some fresh ways of making my busy life more fun, I decided to ask several friends this question. Everyone defined fun a bit differently. However, the idea of fun that people most often noted was time spent with family, friends, or a spouse.

There was one overwhelming commonality for having fun—being active outdoors. Maybe fun is already making people exercise more. Folks noted fun as taking a walk, watching a sunset, water skiing, horseback riding, watching or playing baseball or ice hockey, attending a football game, swimming, gardening, going for a long run, sitting on the creek bank fishing, climbing a mountain, having a picnic when it's sweater weather, and sitting out on the patio late at night with the tiki torches lit and a fire in the chiminea. The latter sounds like my kind of fun!

There were other fun ideas that didn't necessarily require being outdoors, but they did require getting out of the house. This kind of fun was described as going out to dinner, shopping for shoes, attending live music concerts, visiting cool architectural spaces, exploring art exhibits, and going country western dancing. I think my first vote of a fun pastime would be shopping for shoes, with going out to dinner a close second! My daughter voted the same.

But apparently many people also have fun inside the comfort of their homes and sometimes even when they are alone. Folks mentioned such merriments as cooking, taking a Sunday afternoon nap, reading a good book, dancing when no one else is watching, playing with kittens and puppies, surfing the Web, exploring spiritual truths to their depth, as well as doing artwork with grandchildren.

One friend mentioned the excitement she feels every time she sees the beach. I completely relate to the exhilaration and jubilation she feels at the beach. I feel it, too!

Another mentioned traveling and cruising with friends as her idea of enjoyment. Sounds fun to me.

I was captured by the idea one friend shared: "Doing new things but not quite the 'jump off the cliff in my wing suit' level." Did you see *that* YouTube video? I'm quite sure I'm not ready to take flight in a wing suit, but I do love the idea of doing new things and traveling to new places as a preferred choice of recreation and amusement. Or as another friend said it, "Doing something unusual that's not part of my daily routine—letting go of inhibitions."

A couple of friends shared some ideas of fun that may best describe my current longing. One said, "Laughing so hard that tears roll down my cheeks." Another friend summed up fun as, "Anything that gets me to stop thinking and just 'be'—shopping, singing, dancing, laughing, or any combination of those."

Sometimes I think too much about everything that's going on in my life or a family member's life or what's on the news. I want to stop thinking so much and just have fun the way my family does when we're at Disneyworld. When I'm at Disneyworld, I can't stop smiling. My face is usually sore by the end of the day from smiling so much. I also feel a strong inclination to hum or skip. No other place on earth can affect me in this way!

But one very wise friend reminded me that there is always joy to be found in everything. She's right. I thanked her for the reminder. A change in my point of view has often changed my outlook from drudgery to joy.

The idea of having fun may sometimes seem far away or unreachable, especially when we feel too busy to take time to do any of the fun things my friends have mentioned. But I think this could be due to a limited view of what having fun means or under what conditions that fun is supposed to happen. Perhaps we need to broaden and expand our definition. My friends gave me more possibilities of fun to consider. I hope you'll find their list helpful as well.

Finally, in the words of yet another thoughtful friend: "May we all find a little fun whenever we need it." Maybe we could make our own fun by imagining our favorite song playing while we dance up the stairs. I can just imagine my daughter dancing up the stairs on her way to teach a history class. I still remember her doing pirouettes down the grocery store aisles when she was a very young girl. She had on her tiara even then.

Part Five
The rest of your life

141 | Introduction

144 | Trust your highest advisor—your intuition

147 | A wise ruler hears all sides

151 | Comforting those in your domain

153 | Value the wonders in your empire

156 | Royalty is no excuse for arrogance

159 | When your glass slipper is a flip-flop

162 | The supreme response is to forgive

165 | The royal groove

168 | Decree that each day be the best it can be

The rest of your life—Introduction

Could it be that we never learn all there is to learn?

I was asked, "What is something you would learn if you had the chance?" I was stumped. I eventually thought of an answer—to snow ski—but I still can't believe how tough a question this was for me. I wondered why I had trouble coming up with an answer. Surely I could think of more than one answer to such a question. My daughter would have made a long list in probably ten seconds flat.

Throughout our childhood years, the world is our classroom. Our curiosity inspires our sense of adventure and keeps us expanding our abilities and honing our skills. The search to discover our talents seems inexhaustible and exciting.

I've read that entrepreneur Bill Gates attributes his success to his desire to never stop learning. In fact, Gates once said, "Every now and then I like to pick up a copy of *TIME Magazine* and read every article from beginning to end, not just the articles that interest me most. That way you can be certain to learn something you didn't know previously."

I can see how success in life—throughout our life—is connected to our willingness to stay open-minded and teachable.

This means that throughout our lives we continue to ask questions, imagine the possibilities, and stay open to change, improvement, growth, and progress.

One can also see how ignorance leads to fear. People are often afraid of what they don't understand or aren't familiar with—that of which they have no knowledge. Some people are afraid to learn something new if they think it will lead to changes and take them out of their comfort zone.

When people stop learning, stop wanting or trying to learn, or start believing they have nothing to learn, they cease to make progress. Without progress, there is no life, no growth. At the very least, life becomes less interesting.

Perhaps learning is a habit. Like some good habits, such as eating a balanced meal or exercising, we can get lazy or negligent. Our laziness and negligence become bad habits that are difficult to break—but not impossible. I'd like to think that any bad habit could be broken with due diligence and perseverance, and that good habits can be created and maintained in the same way.

Gandhi's words, "Learn as if you would live forever, live as if you would die tomorrow," tell us there is always more to learn and we should digest as much as we can each day. It is never too late to comprehend and master something new. The old adage "practice makes perfect" is always true regardless of our age.

"A wise man...will increase learning" (Proverbs 1:5). Daughters of the world, be wise women. Approach each day with this question: "What can I learn today?" You may not know what you want or need to learn, but I believe there are countless options and infinite possibilities when you're open and ready to discover them.

The essays in this chapter share more of my own illuminating discoveries as well as offer instructive reminders and encouragement as you go about the rest of your life.

Remember, every daughter is her mother's princess. Your castle—your life—is yours to rule. You are royalty and your crown can never be taken away. May your reign be filled with majestic beauty and supreme satisfaction. And may you live happily ever after.

Trust your highest advisor—your intuition

There are times perhaps when "temptation" gets a bad rap. It's wise to keep our wits about us so as not to fall prey to seduction and allurements that would lead us down troublesome paths. But are there times when we're tempted—inclined—to act and don't, when we should have?

I once asked my daughter Jennifer if she ever had such moments. She said her most vivid memory was not taking Italian during her undergraduate degree and not doing a study abroad in Italy. She could have done both but didn't because she didn't want to leave her boyfriend. She said she has always regretted both choices.

I recall a time when I was tempted to introduce myself to a new neighbor but didn't do so for months. When I finally did, we became great friends. I wished I had acted upon my "temptation" earlier.

In the same vein, I remember when I got my first apartment. I found the one that fit perfectly into my budget, but something didn't feel right. I almost didn't sign the contract so I could keep looking. But because I was in a hurry and afraid I might not find another in my budget, I moved into this apartment. Soon afterward, I could not wait to move out.

There have been jobs that I took even though I was tempted not to—and it turned out I shouldn't have. There have been invitations I was tempted to turn down, but didn't—and should have.

In all of these instances, better decisions probably would have been made if only my intuition had been trusted. Whether we call it a hunch, a vibe, or a feeling in our bones, I believe we all have an innate spiritual intuition that points us in the right direction if we only heed it.

What is it that keeps us from listening to our intuitions and following those "good temptations" that would help us make better decisions, figure out when or what to trust, do things that are right for us and others, and live our lives to the fullest?

Some might say a lack of confidence, self-doubt, insecurity, shyness, desperation, and so on. Everything on our list would undoubtedly be rooted in fear—fear of rejection, of being wrong, of being embarrassed, of being humiliated, of making a mistake, or of not being successful or good enough. Listening to our intuition stops fear from clouding our reason.

Many people like to weigh the pros and cons of everything. But my husband often says, "Study long, study wrong," meaning over-analysis of a possible decision or action can lead to second-guessing ourselves to the point of doing nothing. I've often been good at talking myself out of things.

I love the story in the Bible that illustrates to me how Elijah learned to listen to his spiritual intuition. Elijah, the prophet in early Israel, was faced with a life-threatening political situation. He was very distraught and unsure what to do next. Standing on a mountain, he hoped for God to give him guidance. The Bible speaks of a strong wind, earthquake, and fire that came, but God wasn't in any of those. Then there was a "still small voice" (1 Kings 19:11–12).

I think that still, small voice is indicative of our spiritual intuition. Our fears may seem like a strong wind, earthquake, or fire, and these fears tend to confuse our better judgment. But nothing can silence God's voice. We will hear her guidance as we learn to trust our intuitions, our inner voice that will direct us to what is good. My intuition served me well when I gave my husband my phone number after we first met—a practice I did not usually do on a first meeting with a man. But he called the next day, we had our first date the following weekend, and the rest is our sweet history. My intuition was correct when I stopped packing my bags when I was angry with my father-in-law for something he said. My intuition told me to not rush to judgment. After a few hours, not only did I find it in my heart to forgive, but also my father-in-law and I established what would become a completely transformed relationship of mutual respect and admiration.

We are all intuitive thinkers. I believe God made us this way. I have no doubt that you'll find your instincts are correct whether they are telling you "yes" or "no"—to do or not to do. Trust them. Be sure to act upon those "good temptations" that will ensure your life is satisfying and fulfilling.

A wise ruler hears all sides

Living in an age where participation on social networking websites such as Facebook is an active part of our day, we get a glimpse of how many of us are reacting and responding to national and world events. Lately I've been thinking about how quickly we seem to form an opinion.

Indeed, whenever some story hits the airwaves, my Facebook friends get busy sharing their two cents' worth. Now, I'm not passing judgment. I've done the same. But I do try to know better than to jump to conclusions. It's just so easy to make that jump!

Anyone who has ever been reported on or interviewed by some news outlet would probably agree with me when I say that agenda or biased-free reporting is almost impossible to come by. Or at least that has been my experience and observation.

I have been part of a news story many times, and I don't know of a time when some detail wasn't misrepresented or my words weren't misstated. I'm not saying inaccuracies have always had malicious intent. But there have been times when it was obvious that ill-will was the motivation.

I recall when I was in college and participated in a rally for the Equal Rights Amendment. I was shocked and surprised at the misrepresentation that was shown on the evening news—focusing only on some rather outlandish individuals who attended, which gave a wrong impression of the majority who were there. I've been interviewed a few times in my role representing my local church and was surprised how taking something you say out of context can completely change the meaning of your intent.

Consequently, when I read or hear any news story online, in print, or over the airwaves, I'm not quick to assume that all the facts have been gathered and reported accurately. Often, omission is as blatant and purposefully done as what is wrongfully communicated. Both serve the purpose of presenting a biased perspective.

So whether talking to myself, to my husband, to my daughter, or anyone else, I say, "Remember, there's more to this story than we know or have been told."

This type of cautious reasoning when successfully practiced has enabled me to stay calm, keep my mind open, and learn and know the truth in the situation. Furthermore, this practice has kept my emotions under control and not let me draw premature—and therefore probably wrong—conclusions.

The entire first chapter of the epistle of James in the Bible is full of wisdom. Even though James wasn't talking about modern media, for me, this chapter offers some constructive ideas in regard to our perceptions and opinions as well as our communications. I am often amazed at how I can turn to the Bible in search of answers when struggling with anything, and the verses speak to me in some fresh, specific way.

James writes, "But let patience have her perfect work, that ye may be perfect and entire, wanting nothing" (James 1:4). It's become important to me to utilize patience when gathering information on a news event or when waiting for the event to play out. In other words, predictions and fears are not always right, and generally only hindsight offers the most accurate perspective. When gathering facts and details, I've discovered that many sources are better than one in order to obtain the entire story. Since she is a historian, I'm sure my daughter already knows this very well.

A little further into the chapter James writes, "But every man is tempted, when he is drawn away of his own lust, and enticed" (James 1:14). I've learned to watch out for news coverage that pulls at the heartstrings and stirs the emotions. I want to be sensitive to the plight of others and increase my empathy. But it's also important to be certain that the reporting is not trying to sensationalize a story in order to distort the truth to the point of making the truth unrecognizable. Maintaining objectivity is pretty much impossible when emotions guide reason.

He also writes, "Wherefore, my beloved brethren, let every man be swift to hear, slow to speak, slow to wrath" (James 1:19). In our current times, news travels the globe at amazing speed. I'm still awed that I can be in Texas and Google chat with a friend in Jerusalem. While this verse encourages the idea of being informed, I think it is also a warning against jumping to conclusions or letting emotions confuse our reason and judgment—and they surely will do so.

Toward the end of the first chapter, James writes, "But whoso looketh into the perfect law of liberty, and continueth therein, he being not a forgetful hearer, but a doer of the work, this man shall be blessed in his deed" (James 1:25). I believe the idea of looking to "the perfect law of liberty" is telling me to turn to prayer and meditation before forming opinions and responding to what I hear on the news.

In my prayers, I can't ponder and imagine what God sees and knows and not believe that anything is possible, fixable, and recoverable. I can't ponder and imagine God's love for all of her children and not have compassion, acceptance, and forgiveness of those I think are making wrong decisions or behaving inappropriately. I can't ponder and imagine God's power and presence and not have hope, faith, and trust that everything will work out, that progress will be made, and that lessons will be learned, perhaps in spite of all our human failings and harmful actions.

While you and I will probably continue to spend hours of our day on Facebook listening to and reading many news sources, may we always remember that there is more to every story.

Comforting those in your domain

I still beat myself up over words said many years ago when a friend's child died. I was reminded of this when someone posted on Facebook, "People say odd and not helpful things to the grieving. A simple 'I'm sorry for your loss' is really much more appropriate."

Life can change in the blink of an eye. My friend and I shared many breakfasts together, shopping outings, and trips with our daughters. We went from being together every week to rarely ever seeing each other when her daughter (a classmate of my daughter) died.

Time has not lessened my regrets. I still recall the extreme emotions I struggled with when I went to visit her and pay my respects. My heart ached. I could hardly breathe or swallow as I sat on the swing waiting for someone to open the door. It was like a bad dream that I wanted desperately to wake up from. I didn't want it to be true. I didn't want to believe it was.

I had no idea what to say to my friend when she opened the door. I don't remember what I did say. I just remember feeling later that it was wrong or stupid and I wished I had said nothing at all.

I know now that it's very normal to not know exactly what to say or what to do in these tragic instances. In fact, we don't need to feel we should have answers or provide advice. Often, it is better to say nothing. Being there is enough. Our supportive and caring presence is all that is needed.

Not too long ago I did have the occasion to speak to this friend. I expressed my regret for any stupid statements said in her first moments of grief. She told me that she didn't remember anything I said or anything anyone else said to her during those hours. What she did remember was that I was there.

My mamma used to tell me when I was a child, "If you have nothing good to say, say nothing at all." This advice could be applied in scenarios of grief. However, I would tweak it a bit— "When in doubt, say nothing."

Trust me—there probably aren't many good things to say to someone grieving. It is better to say nothing than something that is later regretted.

So, what should we say or do when wanting to comfort friends in grief? Again, the simple "I am so sorry" can be enough. We might add, "I am here for you."

We can be honest and admit we wished we had the right words, but don't. We should always, always listen without comment. We should never disagree with or argue or judge anything a grieving friend says in their first hours of grief. This is something I wish I had understood back then.

I know that I may not be able to change what I said in the past. But I can consider my words more compassionately in the future. I will remember that giving a hug or holding the hand of a grieving friend speaks volumes. Remember, it is our presence that matters most.

Value the wonders in your empire

We human beings have a curious capacity to take things for granted. I've heard it suggested that repetition and time are the culprits that dull our sense of wonder. They say even the most exquisite diamond loses its luster with familiarity or the sunrise fails to astonish because it is commonplace.

There are many things that have, at times, become routine and expected in my life.

Have you ever been in the shower washing your hair, as I have, when suddenly the water stops coming out because city crews have shut down the system for repairs? Or how about when storm damage causes the loss of electricity? Or your car is in the shop and you have no other mode of transportation? Can you remember what life was like before the Internet and cell phones? Or what about the brother you can always count on, or your good health or the many freedoms we enjoy in America? Oh yes, there are many things, experiences, and people I've taken for granted!

One day an email landed in my box that inspired more thought on this subject. It told about a group of students who were asked to name what they thought were the Seven Wonders of the World. The wonders that received the most votes included Egypt's Great Pyramids, Taj Mahal, Grand Canyon, Panama Canal, Empire State Building, St. Peter's Basilica, and China's Great Wall.

But apparently one student had trouble finishing her list, stating she could not make up her mind because there were so many to choose from. The teacher encouraged her to share her list aloud with the other students to see if they could help. She read, "I think the Seven Wonders of the World are to see, to hear, to touch, to taste, to feel, to laugh, and to love."

This unexpected list was followed by a poignant reminder—"The most precious things in life cannot be built by hand or bought by man."

This student listed "wonders" that I never thought much about until one day a few years ago when my husband and I took Shirley, my role model for being a supportive friend in Part 1, for what turned out to be her final jeep ride.

Riding in the jeep was not a big deal to me, perhaps because it was "old hat" as some might say. But Shirley, then in the final stages of her battle with cancer, noticed details I never had and she relished every moment of her ride. I was captivated by her adoration and reverence for what she was seeing and by every breath of fresh country air she took in so gratefully. She passed on a few months later.

My jeep ride with her taught me lessons I will never forget. I discovered colors in the sunset I didn't know were there. I learned that each of our cows has its own distinct bellow and some have really long eyelashes. I noticed that the deeper the hole you drive over, the harder your laugh will be. I found that looking out over big Texas pastures reminds you of the broad expanse of God's love. I was informed that gazing at the horizon when the sun is setting fills you with a peaceful sense of the infinity of life.

How do we keep our sense of wonder? How do we maintain our appreciation of all the everyday miracles that compose our day? How do we never overlook the blessings that make up each life moment?

Even to ask such questions is a good beginning. Pausing to ask these questions also requires pausing to explore for the answers. Our sincere desire to cherish life is a prayer in and of itself—and one that will be answered.

As I learned in my jeep ride, the more acutely aware we are of what and who shares our days, the more meaningful and satisfying life will be. Savoring and mindfully using any of the wonders of sight, hearing, taste, touch, feeling, laughter, and love will guide you to even more of the wonders that God promises for her beloved children.

Start right now—this very moment—and keep yourself in a constant state of awe, admiration, and respect for every ordinary and extraordinary wonder in your day. You don't want to miss anything. I sure hope I don't.

Royalty is no excuse for arrogance

With her master's degrees in English and history, I suspect my daughter knows the meaning of the idiom "Get off your high horse!" I suspect we've all said this—or felt like saying it—at least once in our life.

In short, the demand is to stop acting as if we are better or more intelligent than other people. The call is to become more humble, less haughty, and to lose any attitude of superiority with its overbearing manner and distasteful pride.

This phrase is directed at dismissive arrogance, which I can assure you will poison any relationship—between husbands and wives, queens and their princesses, bosses and their employees, or leaders and their constituents.

The arrogant person assumes her views and opinions are "the truth." She is more concerned about her own viewpoint being heard and obeyed than being right or doing what is right. She demands respect from others when she needs to give respect to others.

An Arabian proverb warns, "Arrogance diminishes wisdom." Indeed, arrogance and pride can keep us from making good decisions.

There was a general named Naaman, whose story is told in the Bible (2 Kings 5:9–14). Naaman's inflated arrogance and pride almost kept him from being healed of leprosy. When he went to Elisha the prophet in search of healing, Elisha sent a message to him telling him to wash seven times in the Jordan River and his skin condition would be cured.

Naaman was disappointed that Elisha had not come to see him in person to perform an amazing show of God's healing power. He reacted with haughtiness and disdain at Elisha's instructions and even asked why he couldn't wash in a different river that he thought was cleaner. But Naaman's servants eventually persuaded him to follow Elisha's directions, and he was cured.

I think the lesson for Naaman (and all of us) is to be willing to listen and humble our ego enough to be open-minded to a new idea—a better and more productive solution than perhaps what we first thought was best.

Have you ever asked someone for advice and then didn't pay attention to it because it was not what you were hoping to hear?

If we want the advice of others, we need to be willing to listen and to be attentive and open to their ideas and suggestions. We need a sincere desire to learn. With that learning, we must be willing to adapt any preconceived notions. This attitude will keep us teachable and no doubt direct us toward wiser decisions.

Even when we are confident about a decision we've made today, we need to be open to making a new one tomorrow.

We live in an ever-changing world. To keep pace in this world, we need to maintain a modest estimate of our own opinion and remain ready and willing to be taught, to be flexible, and, yes, to change our mind.

This may mean taking a different approach. This might require an admission that you've made a mistake. Relationships benefit when we get off our high horse and are not so certain we are right. After all, we might not be.

When your glass slipper is a flip-flop

Can you remember life before flip-flops? I suspect not, since flip-flops are at least six thousand years old! I can't remember a time as a young princess when I didn't own a pair.

In the United States, the flip-flop caught on during the post-war 1950s boom—which explains why I've always worn them, since I was born in the 1950s. Becoming part of "pop culture," flip-flops became a defining example of an informal lifestyle and came to represent the surf culture in particular. Since I am a wannabe beach bum at heart, this is probably one of the reasons I love to wear them.

What I find especially interesting is that the flip-flop has been part of a general overall change in fashion during the past twenty years. Some people call this change the "casual fashion movement."

In the United States, the flip-flop market is estimated at $2 billion retail. It is presumed that most flip-flop purchases are made by those between the ages of 5 and 50, which is roughly a consumer population of 200 million. Since I don't fall within this consumer demographic, I'm here to testify that the flip-flop consumer population is at least 200 million and one.

I have a confession, but my daughter already knows this.

I am a flip-flop-oholic. I am addicted to flip-flops. In fact, I can't get enough of them. One weekend, I bought three more pairs to add to the more than two dozen on my shoe shelves—or maybe there were more than three dozen on my shelves. I don't keep count. But I don't care how many I have. I have no doubt I will be buying more each summer!

I sometimes wonder why I crave flip-flops. Besides the cool and sassy styles, snappy and elegant bling, funky and fancy patterns, and pure, delightful comfort, I think it's the lifestyle they represent that whets my appetite.

I've reached a time in my life when I want to take life a bit slower and easier. I especially want to take most matters less seriously. Informality is something I want in pretty much every area of my life—church, work, travel, meals, or other day-to-day activities.

Now don't get me wrong. I do think "casual" can be taken too far. I still believe there is a right time and place for formality and tradition. I'm not advocating laziness and apathy. Nor am I throwing self-respect aside.

I'm fashion conscious and enjoy dressing in the current trends. Living in Texas, where it's very hot in the summer, I find it's a pleasure to not wear hose and to have a variety of flip-flop styles appropriate for any occasion—from the pool to a wedding. Even within the casual fashion movement, there is still protocol and etiquette on what to wear and when. Yet, whatever the occasion, there's something "footloose and fancy-free" about wearing flip-flops to it. I love anything that helps me maintain a carefree and relaxed attitude.

I wish I had learned how to lighten up when I was a young mother. I think I wasted much time and energy fretting and stressing over inconsequential things. I believe my daughter and I would have been happier without so many rigid schedules. In fact, if I could do young motherhood again, I would opt for more spontaneity and impromptu decisions. If things didn't turn out according to my plans, I would be more adaptable and flexible.

I suspect my daughter is undoubtedly happy to have a more casual and lighthearted mamma these days. My advice to her and all daughters (and mothers) is to avoid being so consumed by schedules and demands that you forget to have fun and enjoy what you're doing. Jobs can be accomplished and done well while still maintaining a sunny and easygoing attitude.

I plan to continue experiencing my simple joy of flip-flops—probably much to my husband's dismay. It's all part of my plan to enjoy life as simply as possible. Life doesn't have to be complicated. Relish the simple joys of life—whatever that means to you.

The supreme response is to forgive

I admit it. I have held a grudge. I'm not proud to say so. However, holding a grudge has never proven to be a good thing in my life.

I've heard that grudge holding is not good for you—it increases stress, raises blood pressure, causes ulcers, and produces a multitude of other harmful side effects. I suspect we all can relate to the lousy way you feel when you're angry with another person.

Holding onto a grudge has generally proven to be the greatest waste of my time and I suspect caused me more grief than it did the person I felt injured by. Holding a grudge never served any good purpose, and it often has cost me a good friend. I've had friendships that never fully recovered, and for that, I'm sad and sorry that I ever let anything permanently hurt my feelings toward a friend.

When I think about where and how some grudges began, I usually can't remember why I took offence in the first place.

Author Mary Baker Eddy has a short essay she titled, "Taking Offense" that I've referred to when I've been irritated by someone's words or actions. She quotes English religious writer and philanthropist Hannah Moore in the opening paragraph: "If I wished to punish my enemy, I should make him hate somebody."

Holding on to resentment, bitterness, hard feelings, or hatred is emotionally draining and physically destructive. So why do we do it?

Once upon a time I felt a friend stuck her nose in where it didn't belong. I not only didn't want her opinion—I disagreed with it. I guess my arrogance took precedence over patience and tolerance. I let myself develop a grudge, and I lost a good friend. Another time with another friend, deep-seated hurt feelings led to my suffering headaches for weeks. I even left the church I attended with this friend because I didn't want to deal with any more confrontations.

In her essay, Eddy says that pride, self-will, and egotism can cloud our reasoning and determine our reactions. But she wisely cautioned, "Well may we feel wounded by our own faults; but we can hardly afford to be miserable for the faults of others."

We can't be responsible for the behavior of others, but we are responsible for how we respond to them. Every action we take has its consequence. As with any action, we should think more carefully about the consequences before we act.

Of course, in any relationship there are times when honest and sincere discussions of feelings are needed. My grandmother advised me when I married to never go to bed angry with my husband. I've not always heeded her instruction, but I have tried. No doubt she got her wisdom from the Bible, "Let not the sun go down upon your wrath" (Ephesians 4:26). This is good wisdom for all relationships—not just with spouses.

Some say it's human nature to hold grudges. Perhaps so, but even still, we always have a choice.

After too many years of making the wrong choice, I hope I've reached a new plateau. I used to brood for days when someone said or did something that hurt my feelings. Not so these days. My efforts to better listen, understand, and empathize with others and their feelings has resulted in my not being too quick to react, over-react, or misunderstand the motives of others.

We can choose to brood, ruminate, and rehash the details of how we've been hurt or disappointed by someone—torturing ourselves by playing the same scene over and over in our heads. Or we can implement a simple, ancient practice—the practice of forgiveness—and dismiss painful memories and move forward.

Life becomes more meaningful and happy by this practice. Hurt and anger should never have the last word. They won't when forgiveness frees you from their venom. It's easier to forgive when I remember I too have need of being forgiven.

The royal groove

Day after day I got out of bed and began the new day. Before I knew it, the day had flown by and I was trying to figure out where it went. Again and again, at the end of the day I was feeling like I would never catch up.

I made myself feel better with the "there's always tomorrow" speech. But eventually I found no solace in those words. I refused to concede that there would never be enough time to do all that I wanted to do with my life. But I was tired of life moving too fast, and I wanted things to slow down.

It occurred to me that perhaps it's not life but rather me that was moving too fast through every moment. If I was the one doing the driving, I was the one who could get out of the fast lane.

"Slowing down" reminded me of a favorite song from my youth: "The 59th Street Bridge Song" by Paul Simon. I started singing its lyrics: "Slow down, you move too fast / You got to make the morning last / Just kickin' down the cobblestones / Lookin' for fun, and feelin' groovy."

Feeling groovy? Those words didn't describe how I had been feeling. I would have loved to make my mornings last. Yes, I definitely needed to stop moving so fast.

I continued to sing.

"Got no deeds to do, no promises to keep / I'm dappled and drowsy and ready to sleep / Let the mornin' time drop all its petals on me / Life, I love you, all is groovy."

Life—I love you? I had not said that in a long time.

I'm not sure I knew what it meant to have the morning time drop all its petals on me. But somehow I liked the way that sounded, and I wanted to find out—especially if finding out would mean everything would be "groovy" in my life.

It was 8:45 in the evening. My morning and day had disappeared yet again. I still had not taken my daily walk. One of my goals had been to walk a mile each day, but way too many days had gone by without my walk. I almost thought, "Another day is done. It's too late."

But then I realized it wasn't dark yet. I bounded out of my house and began my walk.

Suddenly it didn't matter whether or not I walked a mile. So what if I didn't have much time or even enough time to get my mile in before dark. I could still walk!

It's not so hot in Texas right before dark. There was a nice little breeze blowing my hair out of my eyes. The colors of the sunset were barely glimmering in the horizon. The trees surrounding me were becoming dark images. It was like everything was changing from a color photo to black and white—quite an incredible transformation I must say. In those few peaceful moments, any anxieties I had been feeling were replaced with the calming knowledge of a divine ever presence.

I sang, "Ba, da, da, da, da, da, da, feelin' groovy."

I was feeling groovy!

My lesson? Relish every moment of the day. Every minute is important and there to be experienced. If I didn't push so much, it would never be too late. I make way too many rules for my day.

Let's enjoy every moment. May you slow down and be more reflective of the divine in your life throughout your day. I suspect you'll find your royal groove.

Decree that each day be the best it can be

Do you have days you don't look forward to? Or do you have days you dread with every fiber of your being? I recall a day like that. Actually, it was an entire week that consisted of days I didn't want to face.

My husband John had left for a weeklong fishing trip. At the time, we had been married twenty-eight years and this was his first commercial airline flight without me. We had spent relatively few days apart since the day we met.

Although I could handle my fear of being alone and of being separated from him fairly well, I still didn't like it. I didn't relish time apart from him.

Then I listened to a church service webcast. The reader stated a favorite Bible passage in a way that got me to thinking about my days ahead in a fresh light. It was the way he accented the very first word, with a big lift in his voice, which grabbed my attention.

He said, *"This* is the day the Lord hath made, we will rejoice and be glad in it" (Psalms 118:24).

I thought, "This is the day? Today—the day I have been dreading for weeks? How can that be? How can today—of all days—be a day to be happy about?"

But then I reasoned that if the Lord—who is good, who is Love—made each day, then every day must surely have something good about it. I reluctantly conceded this must also include that day, even though when that morning arrived, I thought it was going to be anything but a good one.

When I thought of each day as a day that Mother Love has created for her beloved children, I realized that this day and every day must have purpose, potential, and promise.

I know it's probably normal to be sad when you're separated from the man you dearly love. But I didn't want to spend my time doing nothing but counting down the days until he returned.

I came across a compelling quote that was attributed to Muhammad Ali: "Don't count the days—make the days count." That is what I decided to do that week. I wanted to make the most of every hour of each day. I set a variety of goals that I hoped to accomplish. In fact, I was excited about reaching each goal.

There is great import in valuing each day. When we look forward only to what some future date potentially has to offer, we are probably missing all the options that today is bringing to us. We may even lose or miss out on a great opportunity.

No doubt every day will make its demands of you—some more than others. I believe we can lean on the divine when we're down and depressed, when we're struggling and worried, or when we're uncertain and anxious, and we will be led to exactly what we need. My faith assures me that we can trust and count on it to help us this week and every week.

I stopped fretting about a whole week apart from my husband. I focused on one day at a time. Some days I accomplished projects around the house, other days I met friends for lunch, and I cherished time spent with my mamma. But each day was special, satisfying, and fulfilling. I was never sad or lonely.

So dear daughters everywhere, have a fabulous "rest of your life" and may you make each and every day the best it can be. You rule!

Afterword

I have to share one more thought for all the wonderful daughters (and mothers) who perhaps have reached a time in their life when they are not sure they have accomplished everything they once dreamed of. Dear ones, it's never too late!

What were your childhood dreams?

In search of some fresh inspiration one day, I started reading *The Last Lecture* by Randy Pausch.

The second section of the book is titled, "Really Achieving Your Childhood Dreams." Randy's list of childhood dreams included: "being in zero gravity, playing in the NFL, authoring an article in the World Book Encyclopedia, being Captain Kirk, winning stuffed animals, and being a Disney Imagineer."

What impressed me about his list was its specificity. I asked myself, "What were my childhood dreams?" At this moment, I can't tell you whether or not I've acquired my childhood dreams because I'm still trying to remember what they were.

One of my favorite Disney movies was *Cinderella*, so I'm pretty sure one of my dreams was to find my very own Prince Charming. That goal was definitely reached when I met my husband.

But what other dreams were nestled in my young head?

I remember loving to sing and used to imagine myself making

a record album. I wasn't shy about performing in front of people. I remember going door to door in my neighborhood and asking folks if they wanted me to sing and play my baritone ukulele for them. I was in the school choir and participated in high school musicals. But that's the extent of that dream.

By the time I went to college, I had aspirations of becoming a lawyer and eventually running for political office. But I pushed this dream aside after I met and married my Prince Charming and started dreaming of having children. Oh I know, I could have done both. But I didn't—or haven't yet.

I'm sure I had other childhood dreams that somehow were forgotten and never pursued.

Thinking back on Randy's very specific list, I think his pursuit of dreams was made possible because of his clear and definitive vision of his goals. Even when his specific dream was not exactly realized, his pursuit taught him valuable lessons guiding him in new, often unexpected directions he had never envisioned before.

Basically one could say Randy walked his talk.

Perhaps that is a big key in accomplishing our dreams as well as helping us to not lose sight of them. Got a dream? Go for it! Begin walking the journey. We don't get anywhere unless we venture out. For every dead-end road, there is another road to take nearby. It seems another key in garnering aspirations is being flexible in how we outline our plans so we don't limit the possibilities or our capabilities.

Regarding dreams not achieved, Randy wrote, "Even though I did not reach the National Football League, I sometimes think I got more from pursuing that dream and not accomplishing it than I did from many of the ones I did accomplish." Although he didn't actually "become" Captain Kirk, he did meet his childhood idol years later as an adult. I suspect Randy mastered many of the same leadership skills as Captain Kirk in his own life and profession.

If you're like me and you're having difficulty remembering what your childhood dreams were, don't be discouraged or think your dreams have been lost forever. Start a new list of goals right now. Be specific but remain ready to let your dreams evolve and expand. Then start your pursuit!

Life is about living our goals throughout our entire lives—however small or grand. Day by day and moment by moment, keep pursuing and even adding new ones to your list. Dreaming is not limited to our childhood years, and the pursuit of dreams should never end.

Featured quotes

All Bible passages from the King James Version unless otherwise noted.

- "The art of mothering is to teach the art of living..." Elaine Heffner (opening epigraph)
- "[Hatred] is a plague-spot that spreads its virus and kills at last...if indulged, it masters us." Mary Baker Eddy (p. 17)
- "Only a life lived for others is a life worthwhile." Einstein (p. 23)
- "Greater love hath no man than this, that a man lay down his life for his friends." John 15:13 (p. 23)
- "A friend loveth at all times." Proverbs 17:17 (p. 23)
- "Never go to bed mad." My grandmother (and probably many other grandmothers, too) (p. 35, see also p. 163)
- "Jealousy is the grave of affection." Mary Baker Eddy (p. 38)
- "[Home] should be the centre, though not the boundary, of the affections." Mary Baker Eddy (p. 38)

- "Whatsoever ye would that men should do to you, do ye even so to them." Matthew 7:12 (p. 38)
- "The love of money is the root of all evil." 1 Timothy 6:10 (p. 47)
- "Always be joyful. Never stop praying. Be thankful in all circumstances." 1 Thessalonians 5:16–18 (New Living Translation) (p. 54)
- "Let not your heart be troubled." John 14:27 (p. 60)
- "Fret not thyself." Psalms 37:7 (p. 60)
- "Peace, be still." Mark 4:39 (p. 60)
- "Laugh and the world laughs with you." Ella Wheeler Wilcox (p. 62)
- "Thomas, because thou hast seen me, thou hast believed: blessed are they that have not seen, and yet have believed." John 20:29 (p. 72)
- "Thou wilt keep him in perfect peace, whose mind is stayed on thee." Isaiah 26:3 (p. 76)
- "Yea, though I walk through the valley of the shadow of death, I will fear no evil: for thou art with me." Psalms 23:4 (p. 76)
- "The Lord will bless his people with peace." Psalms 29:11 (p. 76)
- "Whither shall I go from thy spirit? or whither shall I flee from thy presence? If I ascend up into heaven, thou art there: if I make my bed in hell, behold, thou art there. If I take the wings of the morning, and dwell in the uttermost parts of the sea; Even there shall thy hand lead me, and thy right hand shall hold me." Psalms 139:7–10. (p. 77)
- "And the rain descended, and the floods came, and the winds blew, and beat upon that house; and it fell not:

- for it was founded upon a rock." Matthew 7:24–25 (p. 78)
- "Mickey Mouse is, to me, a symbol of independence. He was a means to an end. He popped out of my mind onto a drawing pad...on a train ride from Manhattan to Hollywood at a time when business fortunes of my brother Roy and myself were at lowest ebb and disaster seemed right around the corner." Walt Disney (p. 83)
- "Be not overcome of evil, but overcome evil with good." Romans 12:21 (p. 83)
- "For I know the thoughts that I think toward you, saith the Lord, thoughts of peace, and not of evil, to give you an expected end." Jeremiah 29:9 (p. 84)
- "Cast not away therefore your confidence, which hath great recompence of reward." Hebrews 10:35 (p. 84)
- "Every good gift and every perfect gift is from above, and cometh down from the Father of lights, with whom is no variableness, neither shadow of turning." James 1:17 (p. 84)
- "And ye shall know the truth, and the truth shall make you free." John 8:32 (p. 84)
- "Love your enemies. Let them bring out the best in you, not the worst. When someone gives you a hard time, respond with the energies of prayer for that person." Matthew 5:44 (The Message Bible) (p. 88)
- "The kingdom of God is within you." Luke 17:21 (p. 90)
- "I try not to think about what might have been, cause that was then / There's no way to know what might have been." Lonestar's "What Might Have Been" (p.95)

- "Eye hath not seen, not ear heard, neither have entered into the heart of man, the things which God hath prepared for them that love him." 1 Corinthians 2:9 (p. 96)
- "One man's trash is another man's treasure." Idiom (p. 101)
- "My mom says some days are like that. Even in Australia." Judith Viorst's *Alexander and the Terrible, Horrible, No Good, Very Bad Day* (p. 105)
- "People are about as happy as they make up their minds to be." Abraham Lincoln (p. 107)
- "No man is happy who does not think himself so." Marcus Antonius (p. 107)
- "It is not the place nor the condition, but the mind alone that can make anyone happy or miserable." Roger L'Estrange (p. 107-108)
- "This is the day which the Lord hath made, we will rejoice and be glad in it." Psalms 118:24 (p. 109, 168)
- "The Lord is on our side." Psalms 124 (Holman Christian Standard Bible) (p. 109)
- "The Lord is our strength and song." Psalms 118:14 (www.easyenglish.info) (p. 109)
- "At age 7, Mozart wrote his first symphony. At 12, Shane Gould won an Olympic medal. At 14, Leann Rimes topped the country music charts. At 17, Joan of Arc led an army in defense of Europe. At 57, Ray Kroc founded McDonalds. At 71, Michelangelo painted the Sistine Chapel. At 80, George Burns won his first Oscar. At 104, Cal Evans wrote his first book on the American West." *I Believe in You,* compiled by Dan Zadra (p. 113-114)

- "You lazy fool, look at an ant. Watch it closely; let it teach you a thing or two. Nobody has to tell it what to do. All summer it stores up food; at harvest it stockpiles provisions. So how long are you going to laze around doing nothing." Proverbs 6:6-9 (The Message Bible) (p. 118)
- "The conscientious are successful. They follow faithfully; through evil or through good report, they work on to the achievement of good; by patience, they inherit the promise. Be active, and however slow, thy success is sure: toil is triumph; and—thou has been faithful over a few things." Mary Baker Eddy (p. 119-120)
- "A man's gotta know his limitations." Clint Eastwood as Dirty Harry (p. 121)
- "Jesus avoided energy leaks." (www.heartwiseministries.org/relationship/devotionals) (p. 130)
- "Every now and then I like to pick up a copy of *TIME Magazine* and read every article from beginning to end, not just the articles that interest me most. That way you can be certain to learn something you didn't know previously." Bill Gates (p. 141)
- "Learn as if you would live forever, live as if you would die tomorrow." Gandhi (p. 142)
- "A wise man...will increase learning." Proverbs 1:5 (p. 142)
- "But let patience have her perfect work, that ye may be perfect and entire, wanting nothing." James 1:4 (p. 148)
- "But every man is tempted, when he is drawn away of his own lust, and enticed." James 1:14 (p. 149)

- "Wherefore, my beloved brethren, let every man be swift to hear, slow to speak, slow to wrath." James 1:19 (p. 149)
- "But whoso looketh into the perfect law of liberty, and continueth therein, he being not a forgetful hearer, but a doer of the work, this man shall be blessed in his deed." James 1:25 (p. 149)
- "Arrogance diminishes wisdom." Arabian proverb (p. 156)
- "If I wished to punish my enemy, I should make him hate somebody." Hannah Moore (p. 163)
- "Well may we feel wounded by our own faults; but we can hardly afford to be miserable for the faults of others." Mary Baker Eddy (p. 163)
- "Let not the sun go down upon your wrath." Ephesians 4:26 (p. 163, see also p. 35)
- "Slow down, you move too fast / You got to make the morning last / Just kickin' down the cobblestones / Lookin' for fun, and feelin' groovy." Paul Simon (p. 165)
- "Got no deeds to do, no promises to keep / I'm dappled and drowsy and ready to sleep / Let the mornin' time drop all its petals on me / Life, I love you, all is groovy." Paul Simon (p. 166)
- "Don't count the days—make the days count." Muhammad Ali (p. 169)
- "Even though I did not reach the National Football League, I sometimes think I got more from pursuing that dream and not accomplishing it than I did from many of the ones I did accomplish." Randy Pausch (p. 172)

Acknowledgments

I am not and have never been a college advisor, nor a marriage counselor, nor a divorce lawyer, nor a therapist of any sort. I am my mamma's only daughter and mom to a beautiful and intelligent young woman who happens to be my only daughter. I've been married to the same man for well over thirty years. I've lived in big cities and on a cattle ranch. I've had a variety of jobs in various fields over the course of my life. The wisdom shared in this book comes from many life experiences and lessons, for all of which I'm very grateful.

I am grateful to Carol Hohle of Carol Hohle Communications (www.CarolHohle.com) for her sassy creativity that imagined this book's charming cover along with her many superb design and production skills that brought this book to life.

I'd also like to thank my gifted editor, Laura Matthews of www.thinkStory.biz, for her patience and frankness, which when combined with her careful and precise attention to detail resulted in a meticulously clean and queenly manuscript.

I owe my marketing consultant, Kimberly Proctor of www.CustomersThatClick.com, a heap of thanks for her skillful efforts, masterful advice, and helpful instruction that will surely introduce my books to many more new readers.

I simply must express my thanks to the royally talented, budding photographer Toni Clark for introducing the world to my snazzy and sparkly flare in pictures on this book's cover, my website, social media sites, and more places yet to come.

My life would not be complete without my darling husband John Bridges, the love of my life, to whom I am grateful to have lived with for over half of my life.

My precious daughter Jennifer Bridges is the sunshine and joy in my life, and I am forever grateful to God for allowing me to be her mom.

Then there are the many authors who have inspired me, friends who have encouraged me, my mamma who believed in me, the divine presence I think of as God—not to mention my sweet dachshund—who have unconditionally loved me. My heart overflows with gratitude for them all!

About the author

Author, publisher and women's retreat host, Annette Bridges is on a mission to help every woman realize her story is extraordinary, valuable and noteworthy. She publishes books, journals and coloring books that empower, encourage and entertain. Annette's retreats provide women an oasis to decompress, rediscover their inner child and learn what their hearts desire most.

Before writing books, this former public school and homeschool educator spent a decade writing hundreds of helpful, instructive, and light-hearted columns published by Texas newspapers, parenting magazines, websites and bloggers.

Writing aspirations began as a child with journal keeping, but Annette would not write her first published essay – a guest column in the Dallas Morning News – until she became an empty nester when her only child left for college. Annette went from a brand new empty nest mom wondering what in the heck she was going to do next in her life to a prolific writer.

Annette lives on a cattle ranch with her husband John, dachshund Lady and lots of cows. She can drive a tractor but only if wearing a fresh coat of lipstick and it's not her pedicure day!

You can learn more about Annette's books, blogs and videos as well as her women's retreats at www.annettebridges.com. She invites you to follow her and chat on Facebook at www.facebook.com/TexasAuthorAnnetteBridges

www.ingramcontent.com/pod-product-compliance
Lightning Source LLC
Chambersburg PA
CBHW070611300426
44113CB00010B/1490